A KICK IN THE PANTS
BY JACK POPJES

Blessings!

Jack

Ps 19:7-11

Wycliffe

Partners in Bible Translation

Orlando, Florida
1 800 WYCLIFFE • www.wycliffe.org

Visit Wycliffe's website at **www.wycliffe.org**

A Kick in the Pants
© 2008 Wycliffe Bible Translators, Inc.
P.O. Box 628200
Orlando, FL 32862-8200

ISBN 978-0-938978-46-6

Printed in the United States of America

Library of Congress Cataloging In Publication Data
Popjes, Jack.
  A kick in the pants / by Jack Popjes.
    p. cm.
  1. Christian life--Meditations. 2. Missions. 3. Bible--Translating.
I. Title.
  BV4515.3.P67 2008
  242--dc22
                    2008029108

To order additional copies of *A Kick in the Pants*, contact Wycliffe's Media Resource Center, 1-800-992-5433, *mrco@wycliffe.org*

08   09   01   11   12   13   6   5   4   3   2   1

CONTENTS

PREFACE

"Write what you know" is the first bit of sound advice given to all beginning writers. Howard Klassen may have had that maxim in mind when he recruited Jo and me into Wycliffe Bible Translators.

As a young pastor looking to get involved in cross-cultural ministry, I told him I would like to write articles and books promoting missions and Bible translation. He replied, "Wonderful! Wycliffe needs good writers."

I smiled, pleased that I could embark on a career with Wycliffe as a writer. But my self-satisfied smile dissipated when he added, "Why don't you do a Bible translation program first? Then you'll have something to write about."

That is like saying, "So you want to write about bridge building in Canada. Wonderful! Why don't you design and build a bridge to Vancouver Island? Then you'll have something to write about."

Forty years after that conversation, my first book for a general readership, *A Poke in the Ribs*, was published; two years later, I've completed this one, *A Kick in the Pants*. Howard was right. The 22-year-long Canela translation program in Brazil gave me a wealth of knowledge and experience to share with readers.

It also gave me plenty of experience in three types of writing. Two were difficult but deeply satisfying in the end. The third was easy and fun.

As a para-linguist, I struggled to write technical linguistic papers. The good part was that I could usually use English, but I was in way over my head as I tried to master several theoretical linguistic models to describe the results of our field research to scholars. With plenty of Ph.D. consultant help, I finally managed to publish some material: a 70-page article in a prestigious book on Amazon languages, a tri-lingual dictionary on a computer database, and several articles in

Portuguese describing aspects of the Canela language for Brazilian laypeople who want to learn Canela.

I also struggled to write as an educator and Bible translator. The good part was that I worked on things familiar to me, such as learn-to-read booklets, storybooks, and, of course, books of the Bible. But again I was in way over my head as I struggled to put familiar concepts into unfamiliar language. Were it not for the many fluent speakers of Canela who helped my wife and me, we would never have been able to produce a 770-page, 425,000-word, partial Bible in Canela, as well as 500 pages, worth of educational booklets in Canela and Portuguese.

The third kind of writing, on the other hand, was always a great pleasure. I wrote story-filled personal letters and news reports to our families, friends, churches and other financial supporters. What a relief! At last I could finally write about familiar things, and in my own language at the same time!

A friend once wrote, "Jack, as I came home with a bag of groceries, I brought in the morning mail. Standing by the kitchen counter, I started reading the printed newsletter from you and Jo. I was still reading it when I noticed melted ice cream dripping from the counter!"

That type of positive response encouraged me to write the columns that make up this book.

Not every column contains an anecdote about our family's life among the Canela. Some of the columns tell stories of my childhood, or of my leadership ministry following the completion of the Canela program. All were previously published as weekly columns emailed to over 1,000 subscribers around the world. That is why some columns mention current events and special occasions such as Valentine's Day, Easter and summer vacation.

God developed a unique worldview in me during my childhood in wartime Europe, my teenage years as the oldest son in a poor and hardworking immigrant family in Canada, my young adult years as a student in Bible college and as a beginning pastor, and our child-rearing years as Jo and I lived for decades in an indigenous society. This distinctive but biblical worldview colours every page in this book.

Although I write about a wide variety of topics, every column smells of cross-cultural missions and tastes of Bible translation. I am convinced that the Church's main purpose is to spread the knowledge of the Word of God to every people group on earth. I am confident that the most foundational work any missionary can do is to translate some part of the Scriptures into a language in which God's Word does not yet exist. I am committed to doing what I can to help translate the Bible into every one of earth's nearly 7,000 languages.

I am thankful for the many people who contributed to the articles you will find in this book. God gave my wife, Jo, insight in many areas and the ability to critique my first drafts of Bible translation. She now comments on everything I write. My daughter Leanne brought the fresh pair of eyes that resulted in questions such as, "Did you really mean…?" Over 600 readers of these columns responded via email, some with encouragement, and others with insightful comments, corrections or suggestions for improvement.

I want to give special thanks to Dr. Natasha Duquette, Professor of English Literature at Taylor University College in Edmonton. She assigned two of her best research assistants—students Emily Hollingshead and Eric Franck—to edit the book. They went through the manuscript word for word, correcting everything from spelling to awkward constructions, and standardised the format of the footnotes. The book is now thoroughly Canadianised.

Thanks, too, go to Kristie Frieze, Wycliffe's communications director; to Matt Petersen, who made further editorial suggestions; and to David Bilby, publishing coordinator, who shepherded the process of publishing the book.

Finally, I give thanks to God that I can, at last, "write what I know."

Jack D. Popjes
Sunrise Beach, AB

FOREWORD

I first came across the name Jack Popjes in the 1970s. I was serving on the editorial staff at Wycliffe Bible Translators, USA, when we received an unsolicited manuscript from Brazil with the brash title, "God and the Almighty Dollar."

Whoa! What kind of a title was this, and with audacious expectation that it be printed in the flagship publication of a fairly conservative mission organization? Well, not all of its members were so conservative, that was clear, as this article had been submitted by one of them. But what about the readers? They would be. Or they would think that we were. Or we would rather they think that we were…conservative…most of us…most of the time.

Such is the kind of thinking and second thinking and second thinking after that one can get caught up in. The process is only multiplied when it's a committee making the decision. If you're not very careful, you can come out with plain vanilla every time. That is unless you're very careful not to be very careful!

The fact is, as we read the content under the title, this bold stranger who was bouncing his voice from Holland, to Canada, to South America and now here, made sense. Don't ask me now to recall what it said. I know in the end it all came down to trusting God and not the dollar, but the point was not made without irony, wit, plenty of intended conviction and as I said, plain boldness. We ran the article.

That was my first introduction to Jack Popjes. It was a couple of years more before we actually met, at a two-week-long international conference in Dallas. This time it was me doing the writing, and something I wrote—I don't remember what—attracted him and our in-person friendship began. The only other thing I remember from that time was his often-and-publicly-stated confession that he was addicted to his wife, thousands of miles and still many days distant, and was presently suffering acute withdrawal.

And there it was again…a brash statement, yet not without a certain accuracy, and even something of a testament to marital fidelity.

After that, our encounters were spread around the world with years in between. During those decades, besides reading his words, I had numerous opportunities to hear him speak. And like any good writer, Jack writes like he talks and talks like he writes. Every time he stands to speak, you know he's going to say something bold, likely creative, well-informed—often with statistics and anecdotes from broad reading—sometimes with large doses of self-deprecating humor, clearly audible, and always to the point.

And all of this in English. Of course, you say, but in fact English is not his first language. He's like literary giant Joseph Conrad in this way, a master of a language not his first. But Joseph Conrad did not take a 24-year tour in the jungles of Brazil and learn yet another language, one previously unwritten, produce an alphabet, and grind out a translation of the Christian Scriptures for any in that isolated Canela culture who might want to know what the Bible says and how it might help.

And that little side trip on the road of life, with all of its adventures, misadventures, hardships and faith tests, supplied Jack with a trainload of fodder for considered opinions and fresh insights, the kind which overflow in this book. That's not counting the additional perspective gained from looking at life through the eyes of a completely other culture, or from looking back at his own culture from years spent afar.

But that was Jack's life, and Jo's, and that of their children, whom they raised during all this, supplying yet more material for the mind and the spirit and the pen.

But it goes on. Besides being a writer, a speaker and a linguist, Jack also became a leader in the larger organization he served. Personally, I thought that when the board of directors elected me as executive director for Wycliffe Bible Translators, USA, they had made the most unlikely and risky choice they could have (though I confess I loved the role). But five years later, as I was finishing that up, I learned that the board of directors at Wycliffe Canada had elected Jack Popjes, and I realized that even more unlikely and risky things can happen! (Or so I told him at the time.)

Jack Popjes—who'd have thought?! What will he say? What will he do? What will he write?

Yet the board knew what it was doing. Jack Popjes rose to become one of the most dynamic leaders that the organization has had. If anything, it's a communication job, and Jack was a communicator by blood type. It's a vision-casting job, and Jack leaves a trail of vision behind him wherever he goes. It's a job of creative problem solving, and there didn't seem to be a problem Jack wasn't ready to face with enthusiasm, energy and grit. And it's a staffing job, requiring continual recruitment of scarce personnel to keep all the balls rolling. That's where our roads crossed once again. In the mid-90s, he recruited me.

I wasn't open to his overtures for a long time, but I was a free agent, and he was persistent. It's not that I didn't like Canada (I did), and it's not that I didn't believe in the cause he was trying to address—a new building for a linguistics school. But it was about fund-raising, and by then my heart had turned toward art.

Art!

A strange pursuit indeed in an organization given to science and things more practical. But just the previous year, I'd experienced something quite unexpected—a profound new interest. Art. But how to apply it to anything was the big unanswered question. Later I realized that it was a classic case of the parable where the first servant suddenly found himself the recipient of an out-of-nowhere talent (in that case transferred to him from the one who'd buried his), and was likely left with the motivating challenge to figure out how to fit it into an already full life.

I was in the throes of thinking hard about how to put all this together when Jack Popjes wrote again about this development-director job in British Columbia. I didn't want it, but in fact it was the only path opening up, so I got creative myself and made a counter-proposal. I would accept the role and give it my best, but for three days a week, not five. The other two days I would develop other talents—writing and painting.

I figured they were desperate; they might go for it.

Not only did Jack go for it, along with Dr. Mike Walrod, the school director to whom I'd be answering directly, but Jack affirmed me for setting an example of a person taking charge of his own life, identifying his gifts, and pushing them as far as they might go. Something like that.

In any case, it was another example of an abundant attitude on Jack's part—ready to take risks, to believe in another person, and to trust God for whatever might happen.

As it turned out, I didn't take the writing day, but I did the painting day, once a week. For me, those four years were like returning to college for another degree. In the end, I did become a painter…a vocation I now pursue full time, along with my wife, also an artist with late-developed talent.

It was Jack Popjes who let it happen, who allowed it, fostered it, affirmed it.

And he did it with his words.

There's something about that—creating with words. It's something we do, or can do, out of our shared nature and imitation of God: We create with our words. We speak and things are formed, and nurtured and shaped. It is in this vein I commend to you Jack Popjes, the wordman. Take his words to heart. They come from a great heart, indeed.

Hyatt Moore
Dana Point, California
www.hyattmoore.com

A KICK IN THE PANTS

A swift kick in the pants is always painful, and often instructive. I was ten years old when I got my first kick in the pants. It was my own fault. I was holding my little brother Henkie by the hand as we walked home from school for our lunch break. Suddenly he started screaming as if he had been hit in the face with a whip. He had been!

A boy about my own age, sneering nastily from the other side of the picket fence, raised his metre-long willow switch and was about to strike again. I yanked Henkie to safety and comforted the little kindergartner, aghast at the red weal running from forehead to chin.

This needed to stop, so I walked to the gate, leaving Henkie sobbing, but safely on the sidewalk. I strode up the path and rang the doorbell. An ugly, scary-looking man yanked the door open, glared at me and yelled, "What do you want?" The whip-wielding boy peeked around the corner of the house, and, still sneering, stuck out his tongue at me.

"Sir," I said, "your boy just now hit my little brother in the face with a willow stick." Before I had even finished my sentence, the scary man spat out a stream of violent curses, shook his fist at me and slammed the door in my face.

As we walked home, I wondered what my mama and papa were going to think about the ugly red welt on Henkie's face. I worried I was going to get into trouble for not taking care of him.

We were walking on a wide but crowded sidewalk just a few blocks from home, when I heard running footsteps behind me. Suddenly I felt as if a bomb had exploded under my bum. The impact lifted me off the ground and dropped me on my hands and knees several metres ahead. Henkie started screaming again, several people were shouting. Then, through my tears of pain, I saw the same beastly man who had verbally abused me a few minutes earlier, running away.

I comforted Henkie again, carefully picked the bits of gravel from my bleeding knees and limped the rest of the way home. When I told our story, Papa called the police and, instead of going to school that afternoon, I spent an exciting hour in the police station. When I described the scary man who had kicked me, the policeman nodded knowingly and whispered something to my papa. Then he sat down in front of me, knee to knee, and gave me an instructive lecture.

"You were a very brave boy, but very foolish. You could have gotten badly hurt. If that brute had been drunk, as he often is, he might have killed you. You should have told a teacher, or gone home and told your parents, and let an adult handle this."

Instructive kicks in the pants come in various forms. Twenty-five years later, in the Canela village, I got another kick in the pants. This time it was even more so my own fault.

I was getting myself and my mini-pickup truck ready to drive the four-hour, 70-kilometre trip into town to buy medicines and other supplies. Six people had already asked for a ride and had climbed on with their dogs and cargo.

Then my friend, the village chief, arrived, asking if he could have a ride into town. No problem. We both climbed into the cab of my little truck, the size of an overgrown jeep, and drove to the chief's house to pick up what he had called "a few more things."

To my dismay, seven of the chief's relatives clambered onto the back of the little truck, each one carrying a heavy bag of stuff. I slid underneath the truck and inspected the springs. They were not just flat, but curving down. I had seen that before, just before one broke. No way could I carry that kind of load.

By this time dozens of Canela men surrounded the truck, some of them, no doubt, planning to climb on the back as soon as I drove away. I told the chief that I couldn't carry all his family. "Too heavy," I explained. "The springs will break."

His response was instantaneous, as painful and embarrassing as a swift kick in the pants. He glared at me and angrily ordered his relatives off the truck. Then he and his family marched into his house and sat down, muttering angrily. The Canelas around the truck looked at me as they whispered to each other. I waited a little while, hoping the chief would come out with his personal baggage and climb into the cab, but he stayed where he was. This was not good.

I went in and invited him to come alone or with maybe one or two of his family. No way. He was adamant and beyond cajoling. I knew I couldn't drive away with this issue unresolved. The chief was my friend. He also had enormous influence and could make a lot of trouble for us, so I sat down on the floor with them in silence, and waited, and prayed.

After a long time, a young man came in and whispered in my ear, "The other riders have left." I went out to look, and sure enough, only one old man sat on the truck. Now there was room for the chief, his relatives and their stuff. A few minutes later we were on our way, the chief himself warning people not to climb on the back. "Too heavy," he shouted. "The springs will break!"

As a little kid in Holland, I didn't know any better when, through a kick in the pants, I learned to stay out of adult business. This time I knew better but just wasn't thinking. I was so focused on getting ready to go, I wasn't thinking of Canela culture. I automatically operated on my Canadian "first come, first served" sense of justice and fairness. In the Canela culture, I knew I should have honoured the chief by inviting him first, then those Canelas who worked with us, then our adoptive families, and finally the general public.

Kicks in the pants are usually unexpected, always painful and often instructive. They take many forms from experiences to words, both spoken and written. They come from a variety of sources—even from God. We should heed them, especially the ones God gives us. Sometimes we are so focused on the here and now, a swift kick in the pants is the only way He can get through to us.

❖ Column 2 ❖
Killing the Dream With Love

Cindy may as well have poked her eyes out with her steak knife, cut her leg off with her dad's circular saw or amputated her hand with her mom's meat cleaver. She didn't. She did something even more devastating—she fell in love and got married. Here is her story:

"Ever since I was a teenager, listening to missionaries tell stories in church, I've wished I could be like you. You know, a missionary working in some foreign country," Cindy, the middle-aged mom, told my wife. "But I fell in love with Rob. We married and settled among family and friends. Even now I want to go, but there's no way Rob would ever leave his friends and the business they started. He really loves his work."

We hear these kinds of stories so often, some from men, some from women, each voicing a God-given, long-held yearning—one they should have thought through and acted upon, but didn't. Theologian and storyteller C. S. Lewis describes the yearning that leads to action and results, by writing, "Such longing is in itself the very reverse of wishful thinking: it is more like thoughtful wishing."*

When I speak to young people, I urge them to ask God to give them a life dream, maybe even a dream about doing missions, and then to think of ways to make it come true.

In the sad story of Cindy and Rob, the operative line is, "But I fell in love with Rob." Exactly! That was her problem. Cindy had a life dream, a wish that she longed for but hadn't thought through. She should have done some thoughtful planning like this:

a) I really want to be a foreign missionary.

b) But if I marry someone who doesn't have that dream, I will never be one.

c) So I had better marry someone who also wants to be a missionary.

d) This means I had better not spend time with any guy who is not interested in becoming a missionary,

e) because I might fall in love with him and marry him.

f) Therefore, I will share my dream of becoming a missionary with every guy I hang out with,

g) and refuse to give my heart to anyone who is not excited about my dream.

It is a simple train of thought—not rocket science—but it is amazing how many people do not think this way, and as a result, let themselves get emotionally entangled with someone who will kill their life dream.

Most young people have heard the warnings about alcohol abuse, drug addiction, consumer debt, premarital sex and criminal activities. Getting involved in these life-destroying activities is like jumping off a three-story building. Yes, there is a momentary rush of excitement, but it ends in life as a paraplegic. Strong warnings are in order.

Today's western culture is obsessed with romantic love. The problem is, we hear few warnings against marrying the wrong person.

The Great Dream Giver gives great life dreams to His people, leading to accomplishments that often outlive the dreamer. He wants everyone to live and work to make the dream come true.

No woman plans to marry a man who will murder her. No man wants a wife who will kill him.

To marry someone who does not share your life dream is to marry a dream killer. The one you love will kill your great life dream.

The Dream Giver will be deeply disappointed. So will you.

*Lewis, C. S. "Preface to 'Dymer.'" *Narrative Poems*. Orlando, FL: Harcourt, Inc., 1950, 4.

✦ Column 3 ✦
The Sure Bet

On our fifth day of travel from Alberta to California, while climbing yet another hill on U.S. Interstate Highway 80, an ominous rumbling sound in the transmission announced that our third gear had died. No great surprise, of course. The truck is 18 years old, and our trailer is a heavy, old-fashioned one—some mechanical trouble was to be expected. But we had thought it was worth the risk to make this trip.

The desolate, frozen, January wastelands of northwest Nevada stretched out to the horizon on all sides. Far out of cell phone range, we slowly limped along in second gear for over an hour until we reached a truck stop and a phone. Another six hours later, a tow truck dropped us off in a trailer campground next to a large hotel in Reno. For five full days, while the transmission shop repaired our truck, we lived and worked in our trailer, amid heaps of snow higher than the ones we were escaping back home in Alberta.

For exercise, we walked around in the hotel: up and down corridors, in and out of the boutiques in the hotel mall and the restaurants lining the casino. The casino itself was something to see. We wandered among the acres of slot machines, video lottery terminals, poker tables, roulette wheels, dice pits and horse-race betting booths. We walked while hundreds of people sat, risking piles of money in hopes of getting a major return.

Gambling, apparently, is a growing problem for many people, and not just in Nevada! According to the Canada Safety Council, an average of one problem gambler per day commits suicide in Canada. That is 365 bankrupt, destitute, and now broken, families each year.*

You would think, therefore, that federal and provincial governments would be at the forefront, setting up programs and policies to curb gambling addiction in the same way they seek to deal with drug addiction or drunk driving. There seems, however, to be a conflict of interest.

Critics urge that all video lottery terminals (VLTs) be banned outright, but sadly, governments promote gambling and depend on it. Provincial governments receive a significant percentage of their revenue from the multibillion dollar gambling industry. What's more, a study showed that 35 percent of the province of Ontario's gambling revenue comes from hard-core gambling addicts.

In one year, 2,700 VLTs in bars and restaurants earned the Newfoundland and Labrador government $80 million. Criticism is forcing the government to pass laws to slow the machines down, making them less addictive, and to remove 400 of them.**

Jo and I are gamblers. We take risks, hoping for a great payoff. That midwinter trip to California was important to us. I planned to take a writing course, do lots of writing and some speaking. On the way back, we wanted to see many of our financial supporters and prayer partners. It was worth the risk of mechanical breakdown.

Jo and I are used to risking health, safety, major expense and time in order to accomplish something for God. Following the example of other pioneer missionaries, I took my young family into the jungles of Brazil, and lived in an isolated indigenous village to bring the villagers God's Word in their language for the very first time. It took more than 20 years of our lives. We ran risks and paid the price of snake bites, scorpion stings, rabid dog bites, and every kind of disease from dysentery to tuberculosis. But the payoff was worth it!

Jo and I tell people, "To evangelize the world and disciple the nations, don't be afraid to take major risks!"

Jesus said, "Surely I am with you always, to the very end of the age" (Matthew 28:20, NIV).

Did Jesus lie when He said this?

I am betting my life that He meant it. It's a sure win.

*"Put curbs on casinos, safety council urges." CBC OnLine News. 16 Dec 2004. http://www.cbc.ca/canada/story/2004/12/16/safety-gambling041216.html.

**"Province orders removal of VLT stop button." CBC OnLine News. 23 March, 2006. http://www.cbc.ca/canada/newfoundland-labrador/story/2006/03/23/nf_stop_button_20060323.html.

⊹ Column 4 ⊹
Jesus and the Giant Scissors

When God chose to reveal Himself to people, He decided to use human language, and in so doing, opened a huge can of worms.

The problem with languages is that they are alive. Just like living, growing trees, it is the nature of languages to grow, develop and change over time. It should be no surprise, therefore, that translations of the God-revealing Bible done hundreds of years ago are more difficult to understand now than when they were first translated.

When I was a little boy growing up in Holland, most church-going Dutch people had the custom of reading some Scripture after the main meal. My papa read from the Bible in an old translation, completed over three hundred years before. Naturally the modern Dutch we spoke in school and at home was markedly different.

One day, Papa read about Jesus preaching to a giant pair of scissors. At least that is the picture that popped into my mind. The old 1619 Dutch word for great crowd was *groote schaare*, which sounded to me like the word *schaar*, the modern word for scissors. Thus I understood *groote schaare* to be a giant pair of scissors.

Not only do all languages tend to change, but also the more a language is used, the faster it changes. Since more people, in more countries, speak some variety of English than any other language, it is no surprise that English is changing fast.

That is one reason translators keep churning out so many different translations and paraphrases of the Bible in English. Critics contend that there are too many already, and they may have a point, but translations do need to be upgraded to keep up with changes in the language that people are speaking.

Outdated biblical language can give rise to funny situations. A six-year-old recited the Lord's Prayer at a church service this way: "And forgive us our trash passes, as we forgive those who pass trash against us."

After reading the story of the coming of the Holy Spirit at Pentecost to her Sunday school class, a teacher had children draw pictures of the story. Most of them drew people with little flames dancing above their heads. But one boy drew a group of people packed in a room, into which a car was also jammed. The vehicle was a Honda, apparently, since the little "H" symbol showed clearly on the hood.

"Why do you have a car in the picture?" the teacher asked him. "There is no car in the story."

"Yes, there is," he replied. "You read, 'They were all with one Accord, in one place.'"

My earliest cross-cultural missions experience was in the Yukon, in north western Canada. For several months my ministry partner and I held church services in a village of indigenous people. They spoke their own Kaska language among themselves and English with us.

I preached and taught informally, both answering and asking questions during my sermons. I read to them from the King James Authorized Version. From the questions I fielded, I was convinced the Kaska people did not understand it. How could they, since modern English was not their heart language, and the KJV translation was 350 years old?

Not being an immigrant who had needed to learn English on the fly, my colleague had never experienced the frustration of hearing words and not understanding them. He just wanted to read the old King James Bible slowly, clearly and expressively, over and over again, and believed the Kaska speakers would eventually understand it. I doubted it then and doubt it even more strongly now.

I was part of a team promoting Bible translation at Amsterdam 2000, where the Billy Graham Evangelistic Association had convened 12,000 evangelists from all over the world. Scores of theologians worked to develop the "Amsterdam Declaration." It clearly states the importance of Bible translation.

The declaration states, "We must proclaim and disseminate the Holy Scriptures in the heart language of all those we are called to evangelize and disciple. We pledge ourselves to…remove all known language and cultural barriers to a clear understanding of the gospel on the part of our hearers."

This is a far cry from repeatedly, clearly and expressively reading a Bible translation that is 350 years out of date to a group of people who barely understand modern English. Faith comes by hearing—the hearing of the Word of God. This biblical truth implies hearing it with understanding, which means that we must hear or read the Bible in the language that we know best.

It is great to know that speakers of nearly 3,000 languages can hear or read at least some of the Bible with good understanding. No more Jesus preaching to giant scissors!

What's more, Bible translation programs—many staffed by nationals who are translating into their own language—are currently active in nearly 2,000 more languages. That adds up to almost 5,000 languages with either an existing translation of some Scriptures or an ongoing translation project.

There is good progress being made in dealing with that can of worms, even though speakers of about 2,000 languages are still not able to understand God's message to them.

They continue to wait for the Word of God to be translated into their own language.

✧ COLUMN 5 ✦
THE ATHEIST WHO PICKED
THE RIGHT TARGET

Atheists, in general, are a wrongheaded bunch, but this one in Italy got something right.

Luigi Cascioli, a 75-year-old, life long atheist, said, "Enough is enough," and is now suing a local parish priest, and by extension, the whole Roman Catholic Church. The basis of his suit is that Jesus Christ is an invention—that He never existed. The Church, he alleges, is therefore guilty on two charges under Italian law: the abuse of popular belief, a charge normally levied against swindlers and con men, and impersonation—substituting one person for another.

Never mind the arguments in North America about evolution versus intelligent design; this month an Italian court is going to tackle the issue of Jesus Himself, examining the evidence as to whether He ever existed. Luigi claims the Church invented Jesus, basing Him on John of Gamala, a first-century Jew who fought against the Roman military dictatorship.

Atheist Luigi got it right. He aimed at the right target. Jesus Christ is the greatest argument for the existence of God. His supernatural birth, His perfect life, His death—foretold in detail—and His unexpected resurrection, if true, are the final answer to every atheist's objection. On the other hand, if Jesus never existed and none of these elements are true, then the Church has lied, and lied, and lied, steadily for 2,000 years, and it is about time to put a stop to it.

All very logical.

I don't know what the verdict of the court will be. Certainly there is plenty of extra biblical evidence to show that Jesus not only existed, but also that He lived, died and rose again from the dead exactly as stated in the four records of the biblical evangelists.

I do wonder what brought on this charge. What kind of Christianity is Luigi familiar with? A religion steeped in ancient traditions, ceremonies and liturgies? A Church priding itself on massive cathedrals and ornate altars? A Church fixated on political and economic power?

Would he have become an atheist if he had been part of a loving fellowship of Christ followers? What if he had seen Christians sacrifice their careers and personal ambitions, not to gain their own salvation, but to work for the salvation of others? What if he had seen and experienced the power of the Holy Spirit to bring physical, emotional and spiritual healing?

People all over the world—atheists and everyone else—desperately need to see and experience Jesus Christ living through His followers. Holy Spirit-empowered Christianity has nothing to do with political and economic power, nor with massive buildings, organizations or programs. The reality of Jesus may well be shown more clearly in the back of some cave, where a handful of persecuted Chinese Christians huddle together, encouraging one another, than in a stadium packed with North American churchgoers cheering a big-name speaker.

Jesus Christ is central to the Church, to the future of planet Earth, and to the universe. By Him all things hang together. Deleting Jesus is like deleting the sun from our solar system.

Nice to know that no matter what that Italian court's verdict is, Jesus not only existed 2,000 years ago, but He is also alive and well today, and will be forever. Someday, everyone—even Luigi Cascioli—will kneel to acknowledge that Jesus exists and that He is the master of the universe.

All the more reason for us to keep on building His Kingdom, translating His Word into every language in the world.

"The Atheism of Luigi Cascioli." http://www.luigicascioli.it/ateismo_eng.php.

"Italian Lawyers Asked to Prove Jesus Existed." Associated Press. 21 January, 2006.
http://www.foxnews.com/story/0,2933,182341,00.html.

Dances in Underwear

"Jack, you shouldn't let those Canelas paint you up like that!" a friend from another mission agency exclaimed. "Why do you participate in their ceremonies? You may be opening yourself to demonic influences. As a Christian, you should be staying away from those pagan practices."

He was looking at some pictures of Jo and me, painted red with ochre seed paste.

"We want to be accepted by them," I tried to explain, "so we need to take part in their ceremonies."

Our missionary friend was not the only one who criticised us for identifying so closely with the Canelas. National pastors and other Christian friends also could not understand why we would participate in such uncomfortable, embarrassing and questionable activities.

Long before Jo and I set foot in the Canela village, we prayed, "Lord, we don't care what it costs us. We don't care how long it will take, or what we have to go through. Please use us to bring these Canela people Your Word in their language."

Accordingly, we took Paul's example, who testified in 1 Corinthians 9 that he adapted himself to societies and individuals so that he might bring at least some of them to God.

That is why our family lived as much like the Canela people as possible. We ate and slept in a palm-thatch house with an earth floor and dried mud walls, just as they did. Like our neighbours, we cooked over a wood fire and ate the same wide variety of roots from the fields, fruits from the forest, and animals killed by hunters. Our furniture was homemade, much like theirs, and like the Canelas, we and our girls dressed in a minimum of clothes. I did not dye my blonde hair black, but did let the Canelas cut my hair in their style.

By living like the Canelas in every possible way, the important exceptions stood out. We boiled our drinking water during the rainy season. We used soap and made it available to the Canelas. We treated ourselves and the Canelas with modern medicine, and prayed for their healing. Jo and I did not participate in the sexual free-for-all during the opening and closing days of the festival season. We carefully picked the areas where we acted counter-culturally, but in everything else, we lived like the Canelas.

After some years, having become more fluent in the language, we studied the Canela body decoration designs, the materials used and the purposes of body painting. Black dye, resin and charcoal, and, of course, the greasy, smelly red ochre paste dye that contaminated everything we touched: furniture, clothing, bedding, paper and books. We were fascinated with the intricate designs and learned about the numerous reasons for decorating the body.

That's when we discovered that the main reason for using red ochre dye was to repel "them"—the demons and harmful spirits that were not talked about. Aha!

I could hardly wait until the next festival season. When the Canelas came to paint me, greasy ball of red ochre dye in hand, I said, "I don't need any ochre."

"Why not? Are you leaving the village before the festival starts?"

"No, I'll be here for the festival."

"Then you need to be painted up with ochre, or…or 'they' will get you."

"No, I'm not afraid of 'them,'" I explained. "The Good Spirit of the Great Father in the Sky lives in my body and protects me against 'them' from the inside out."

Within hours that news swept across the village. During the festival the next day, our pale skins contrasted starkly with the red bodies all around us—the message now visual, as well as aural. The explanation kept going around, "They are not afraid of 'them,' because the Good Spirit of the Great Father in the Sky lives inside their bodies and protects them."

Sometimes we need to do uncomfortable things, and things we don't fully understand, to bring praise and glory to God. We may be criticised for it—King David was. On the day he brought the Holy Ark back to Jerusalem with great celebration, David put aside his kingly robes. Then, wearing minimal clothing, he danced before the Lord with all his might (2 Samuel 6:14-20). David's wife, Michal, who had stayed home and not taken part in the festive parade, criticised him sharply.

I am not saying that next Sunday we should encourage our pastor to step away from the pulpit and dance before the Lord in his underwear—nor that any of us should do so.

What I am saying is that we should not let potentially difficult situations keep us from getting involved in meeting the world's needs. All around us are hurting people and marriages in trouble: adults and teens enslaved by substance abuse, men trapped by pornography, families abandoned by one of the parents. Stories of global poverty, genocide, violence and every sort of human suffering fill the newscasts. There are 200 million people speaking 2,000 languages in which not one verse of the Bible has yet been translated.

All these needy situations are opportunities for Christ followers to get involved. We are overwhelmed with all the ways in which we could advance the Kingdom of God and bring glory to Him. But to do so, we will need to step out of our comfort zone, or make a personal sacrifice, or do something that might draw criticism.

We need to go way beyond the standard "missions as usual" formula of Pray, Give and Go. Instead, we need to commit to *do whatever it takes*.

Few of us will end up with our bodies smeared in greasy red dye, or publicly dancing in our underwear, but to advance the Kingdom of God, we must be willing to do so.

✦ Column 7 ✦
Got Huge Problems?
Ask Kids to Pray

When God installs Himself in the body and life of a believing child, He installs the full, professional version. There is no "Holy Ghost Lite" for kids.

We saw this with our own eyes during the fall of our second furlough, when a mail strike left us without income—there were no online electronic bank transfers back in those days. We all prayed. I prayed for money to pay the rent, Jo for grocery money, and our three school-age girls prayed for winter clothes.

We found affordable thrift store winter boots for Cheryl and Valorie, but none to fit our ten-year-old middle daughter, Leanne. Each night she prayed, "Lord Jesus, I need some snow boots before winter. I'd like a pair of those tall brown ones, please. You know, the kind with the zipper up the side." She prayed this nightly for several weeks, but we found no boots in our price range for Leanne.

One night the weather forecast was for snow, and at her bedside, Leanne prayed, "Dear Jesus, they say You are going to send snow tonight, but You haven't sent me my snow boots yet. Please send me some tall brown ones. You know, the kind with the zipper up the side."

Later that night, as Jo and I wondered what to do, a couple from the church we attended stopped by for a brief visit. The husband handed me a cheque, saying, "With the mail strike, I'm sure you can use this." I glanced at it and thought, "Ah, rent money!"

Then they had to leave. As they were walking to their van, the wife turned and said, "By the way, our daughters are a few years older than yours and they have outgrown some clothes. Would you like a box full of used clothes?"

Did we! I helped the husband carry in a huge box. I know I said "Thank you," but Jo and I were so excited I don't even know if we said "Goodbye." As soon as the door closed, we ripped open the box, and there they were, right on top! I grabbed them, ran down the hall, banged open the bedroom door, flicked on the light and yanked off the covers. Leanne woke up with me stuffing her bare feet into some winter boots. She stood up, rubbing her eyes, and exclaimed, "Winter boots! They fit! Tall brown ones! And look, hey have a zipper up the side!"

God does not come in a child-sized edition. He moves into every believer's life in full, industrial strength. What's more, children have the advantage of freedom from the doubts and fears that often plague adults. As Jesus said, "Unless you return to square one and start over like children, you're not even going to get a look at the Kingdom, let alone get in" (Matthew 18:3, *The Message*).

It is that same child like faith that pleases God when someone starts to believe in Him. When God begins to operate in the life of a new believer, He does so in His full power. It doesn't matter if the new believer is a highly educated university professor or an illiterate child in a mud hut.

We older, more experienced believers need to adjust our superior attitude towards children, new believers and Christians from oral tradition societies. It may well be that God's Spirit is less hindered in their lives than in ours.

Some of us older folk may need to return to basic Christianity by learning from children, like our ten-year-old daughter, who pray consistently, expecting an answer and continuing to trust God even when He delays.

We need to pray for everything, whether it is for healing from illness, for wisdom in making decisions, or for tall, brown snow boots—you know, the kind with the zipper up the side.

LOVE PEOPLE, USE THINGS

"Love people, use things" is not just common sense advice—it is a biblical command. I thought I was living by this maxim, until one day I lost "My Pen of Distinction."

Shortly after my wife and I returned to Canada, having completed the Canela Bible translation project in Brazil, a friend gave me a top-of-the-line ballpoint pen. Not a chrome one (I already had one of those), and not merely silver, but plated with 14-karat gold. A fine gold pen—truly a Pen of Distinction.

It shone in my shirt pocket and gleamed in my hand as I used it every day. It didn't improve my handwriting, but it sure looked good in my fingers. When I sat for a set of official portraits as CEO of Wycliffe Canada, I held it in my hands, the gold matching the black onyx gold ring and tie clip my wife had given me. Yes, I valued My Pen.

How much I loved it became even clearer when one day I could not find it. I thought I might have lost it at church where, each Sunday, I used My Pen to take notes of the pastor's sermon. I went back to the church the next day and crawled under the pews where I had been sitting, looking everywhere. But My Pen continued to be lost.

I even asked the church secretary to put an announcement in the church bulletin about My Pen being lost, and she did. Weeks later, during a cleaning binge at home, My Pen and I were reunited when I found it deep inside a sofa. What a relief!

A week later, I lost it again, hundreds of miles from home. Someone eventually found My Pen, however, and mailed it back to me. I was ecstatic as I slid My Pen out of the package and fondled it. In fact I was so happy that I sat and thought about it for a while and realized there was something wrong.

As a pioneer Bible translator, I had done my life's work writing with a pencil on the back of old newsletters, while sitting on a stool in a palm-leaf hut with a dirt floor. After living for decades with very few material things, I thought I would be immune to loving things. But now I began to wonder. My Pen was very special. It had been given to me by a friend. It cost $75 and I would never buy one for myself. And I really liked the way My Pen handled, wrote and, being gold, how elegant it looked in my hand.

At that point I realized I didn't own My Pen—My Pen owned me. I used it, yes, but I also loved it.

My love for My Pen forced me to use the church secretary, who went to extra work and effort, to try to find it.

I used my wife to listen to my frustrations as I grumbled and stomped about the house looking for My Pen.

My relationships with my family and co-workers suffered as my thoughts kept returning to My Pen, while it was lost.

"Let's face it, this beautiful pen is making me sin," I muttered, as I thought of my failures.

I took a deep breath, used My Pen to write a short note, then slipped the note and the pen into a padded envelope and sent it away to a friend as a gift.

Did I give my beautiful gold pen away while in the grip of a raging fit of uncontrolled generosity? No. Getting rid of it was as coldly deliberate as reaching for my bush knife and whacking the head off a poisonous snake that had threatened the life of one of our little girls.

"If your hand causes you to sin, cut it off….If your eye causes you to sin, pluck it out," Jesus said (Mark 9:43, 47, NIV).

"If your pen causes you to sin, give it away."

Hey, I think I got off easy.

POLISHING ALL THE FACETS

"For the first few years of our marriage, I felt my husband's role was to provide the money I wanted to spend." I smiled when my colleague told me this—but she wasn't joking.

Her comment reminded me of a roughneck I worked with in the oil field as a teenager. He told me about his marriage, graphically describing how his young wife fulfilled her role in the sexual side of marriage. "That's the main thing she is there for," he assured me. He wasn't joking either.

Both of these marriages were sick and unbalanced. Healthy husband-and-wife relationships are multifaceted and complex, like a well-cut diamond. A typical diamond is cut with 58 facets—33 on the crown and 25 on the pavilion. When they are uniform and symmetrical, they refract and reflect the light, dazzling the eye with their beauty.

It would be the height of insanity to cut and polish only half-a-dozen facets on a diamond. It would look terrible. What a waste! So also with a marriage that focuses on only a few aspects and neglects the rest.

My colleague's husband needed to fulfil his role as provider, but that was not his only role. The roughneck's young wife certainly was there to satisfy her husband's need for sex, but that was not her only role.

There is also companionship, mutual communication, helping each other make good decisions, encouraging each other, helping each other to get back up after a stumble, and working together as a team, as parents and as leaders in the home. Who knows how many roles there are? Maybe there are as many roles in a marriage as there are facets to the diamond on the wife's finger.

Diamonds and marriages both need to have every facet cut and polished to bring out the beauty inherent in each.

So it is in our relationship with God.

God is our Helper in time of trouble. But if the only time we call on Him is when we are in trouble, the relationship is not in good shape.

Our relationship with God is vast and complex, with so much potential it is impossible to describe in abstract terms. The Holy Spirit uses dozens of metaphors to give us a few glimpses of the reality of this relationship.

God is the Creator; we are His creation. He is the Potter; we are the clay. He is the Shepherd; we are the sheep. He is the Rescuer; we are the lost. He is the Master; we are the slaves. He is the Owner; we are the owned.

These pictures focus on our total helplessness—mere clay in the Potter's hand. The problem is that a healthy relationship with God is not possible by focusing only on this aspect of helplessness and dependence. It breeds apathy and fatalism.

To bring balance, the Bible also presents God as Boss, and we as managers in building the Kingdom. Jesus is the Great Shepherd, and leaders of the Church are under-shepherds. Christians are co-labourers together with God.

Yet another facet of our relationship shows God as our loving heavenly Father, and us as his beloved children. Quite a contrast with the Master-slave situation.

During His last day on earth, Jesus revealed yet another aspect of God to his disciples: "I'm no longer calling you servants because servants don't understand what their master is thinking and planning. No, I've named you friends because I've let you in on everything I've heard from the Father" (John 15:15, *The Message*).

The most shocking metaphor, however, is of God as the Lover and Christians as His beloved.

In the Bible, we are called the bride of Christ. A groom loves his bride, and the bride loves him back. Just as spouses in a healthy marriage seek to please each other, so Christ, the Groom, and His bride, the Church, bring each other unimaginable joy. What a picture! From clinging clay to beautiful bride, and everything in between.

Yes, we are mere clay, but we are also His bride. We are slaves, but we are also His children. We are dumb sheep, but we are also His friends in whom He confides.

All these pictures are true; so are dozens more. But if we pick out one or two, and focus only on them, we damage our relationship with God. Cults start this way, and so do holier-than-thou movements. Our relationship with God would be like that of the wife who saw her husband as an unending supply of money, and the roughneck who used his wife only for unlimited sex.

The only way we can be thoroughly familiar with all of these Holy Spirit-inspired metaphors is to read the Bible. Which reminds me: There are still at least 190 million people, speaking thousands of languages, who do not have a Bible in their language.

How are they going to develop a relationship with God that goes beyond Creator-creature? God wants them for His bride.

They don't even know there is going to be a wedding.

⟡ Column 10 ⟡
"What About Me?"

"What about me?" our four-year-old grandson, Aidan, would ask when he saw people preparing to go somewhere or getting ready to do something exciting.

When he and some of his cousins had a sleepover at Grandpa and Grandma's house, he would listen carefully to be sure that my bedtime story included a boy about four years old. If it didn't, he would look up at me in consternation and ask, "What about me?" and I would hastily add a character that closely resembled young Aidan.

We expect questions like this from a four-year-old. It's natural and normal for a small child to be self-absorbed and to feel that the universe rotates around him. It is disgusting, however, when mature adults, ten times Aidan's age, display an "It's all about me" attitude. Life is not about me. It is not about you. It's not even about other people.

You would think that Bible-reading, church going Christians would know better. But no, the same attitude prevails among many Christians. On second thought, that's not surprising. Do you ever listen critically to some of the new worship and testimony songs? I heard one the other day: good tune, solid biblical lyrics about Jesus leaving heaven and coming to earth to die in agony on the cross. Then came the chorus, "He did it all for me." Hold it!

He did it all for me? No, He didn't! For starters, He died for the whole world—for billions of people. The world's best-know Bible passage starts, "For God so loved the world...." Jesus paid the price to redeem all of humanity, and the rest of the cosmos, too. Yes, I am part of that *whole world,* and so are you, but His motivation in dying on the cross was not to save me, or you, or anyone else. He died to accomplish a much greater goal than that.

When we begin to trust Jesus, we come into a new and living relationship with the God of the universe. That's great, but it's still not the end goal. The whole point of the plan to save mankind and restore the rest of creation is ultimately for us to love God, to enjoy Him, to please Him, and to *make Him look good*. In biblical language, to glorify Him.

Paul used the term, "…that we…might be for the praise of his glory" (Ephesians 1:12, NIV). Paul's counsel was, "Whether you eat or drink or whatever you do, do it all for the glory of God" (1 Corinthians 10:31, NIV).

It is all about God. He created us, brought us into this world, and gave us spiritual life so that we would glorify Him by loving Him, enjoying Him, pleasing Him and worshiping Him.

"God is the most self-centred Being in the universe," an atheist friend once exclaimed during a discussion. That's not blasphemy. It's not criticism. It is glorious truth.

God knows that He is the One who holds everything together; but that's not enough. He wants everyone—humans, angels, demons and every being in Heaven, on earth and in Hell—to realize that He is the Centre of everything.

When we love someone devotedly, we put him or her in the centre of our lives. That is why the first commandment God gave Moses is, "Love the Lord your God with all your heart and with all your soul and with all your strength" (Deuteronomy 6:5, NIV). Beings—human and otherwise—who love God put Him at the centre of their lives; they recognize that He is the Centre of everything.

God does not command us to do anything He is not already doing Himself. He knows He is the Centre of everything. He wants us to know. God is devoted to Himself; He cannot be otherwise. If He did not love Himself, He would no longer be the Centre of everything, and, like an off-centre flywheel, the entire cosmos would fly apart. He commands us to join Him in loving Him, in being devoted to Him, and to think, speak and act only to please Him.

That is why those great heavenly worship scenes described in Revelation are so stirring. At last, everyone is worshiping and glorifying God—not just the angels in Heaven, but also every being in the universe.

That's why it is so right to obey Jesus' command to evangelize the world and disciple the nations. That is why Bible translation is so foundational to bring glory to God. God wants people from every language and nation to make Him famous.

That is why we continue to call people to give up self-oriented lives and focus on pleasing God.

No, Aidan, it's not about you. It's not about me. It's all about God.

✦ Column 11 ✦
This Will Happen

No one knows the "when," but here's the "what" of Jesus' return.

Check out what Jesus Himself said in the Popjes paraphrase of Matthew 25:31–46.

Here's what will happen!

When I finally arrive, blazing in beauty and with all my angels, I will sit on my glorious, kingly throne. Then I will call for all the nations of earth to stand before me, and I will sort the people, much as a shepherd sorts sheep and goats, putting the sheep to his right and the goats to his left.

Then I will say to those on my right, "Enter, you who are blessed by my Father. Take what's coming to you in this kingdom. It's been ready for you since the world's foundation. And here's why:

"I was a member of a minority people group whose traditional way of making a living was lost because of socioeconomic pressures from the national culture. I was weak and starving, unable to care for my family. Then you brought me food and taught me how to cultivate the land to raise crops and livestock for food.

"I was thirsty, and all the villagers were sick with diarrhoea, because our water supply was polluted. Then you came and taught me to boil my drinking water. You helped me dig a deep well for clean water and taught me to care for it.

"I was ashamed of being who I was. I may as well have been stark naked in public. The people from the main culture laughed at me when I spoke my language, deriding it as the grunting of pigs. They called me a dumb native, and when they weren't cheating me, they ignored me. Then you came and lived with me. You treated me as a real person, and told me that my Creator loved me. You learned my language and made it a real language, a written language. You strengthened my self-esteem and restored my pride in being who I was.

"I was a stranger in my own land. People from the national culture took advantage of the fact that I didn't know their language and their customs. They cheated me in the marketplace, because I couldn't read the prices. Then you came and taught me to read numbers, to count, add and subtract. You helped me learn how to read in my own language and later in the national language. Now I am treated as a citizen.

"I was sick, my body filled with disease. My emotions were chaotic, and I couldn't cope. My spirit was oppressed with the fear of evil all around me. Then you came and you lived with me, treating my body's illnesses and praying for me. My body grew strong again. You helped me to trust the Creator, who loved me. My spirit received new life, new love and a new power over all the evil around me.

"I was in prison, peering through the bars of my culture at the national culture, which I did not understand and which rejected me. I was handcuffed by my own language. I could not read the message of love my Creator had left for me. Then you came, you learned my culture and my language, and you translated our Creator's message to me into my own mother tongue. At last I could understand. You built a bridge of understanding between me and the foreign culture all around me."

Then those on the right are going to say, "When did we ever see you in any of these desperate circumstances?" Then I will say, "I'm telling you the solemn truth; whenever you prayed for, or gave to, or got personally involved in doing any of these things for someone overlooked or ignored, that was me—you did it to me."

Then I will turn to those on my left and say, "Get out, you worthless egocentrics. You're good for nothing but the fires of Hell. Here's why: I was in desperate straits in every way: physically, emotionally, socially and spiritually. Yet you did nothing to help me."

Then they will say, "When did we ever see you in such desperate circumstances?" Then I will say, "I'm telling you the solemn truth; whenever you refused to help someone who was being overlooked or ignored, you refused to help me."

Then I will send those on my left to their eternal doom and take those on the right to their eternal reward."

This Will Happen.

Statistics on world need:

- Nearly one billion people have no way to feed themselves adequately. They go to sleep hungry every night.
- Every day, more than 16,000 children die from hunger-related causes—one child every five seconds.
- Nearly 3,000 children die every week from lack of safe drinking water and adequate sanitation.
- One billion adults have never had the chance to learn how to read.
- More than one billion people speak a minority language as their mother tongue and live in a depreciated culture.
- One billion people are locked into a world religion that keeps them from the Bible on pain of death.
- One quarter of a billion people speak languages into which not one verse of the Bible has yet been translated.

Hunger:
- www.bread.org/learn/hunger-basics/hunger-facts-international.html
- www.wfp.org/english/

Thirst:
- www.who.int/water_sanitation_health/mdg1/en/index.html
- www.worldwatercouncil.org/index.php?id=23

Literacy:
- www.worldlit.ca/facts.html

Minority languages:
- www.ethnologue.com/ethno_doc/distribution.asp?by=size

World religion:
- muslim-canada.org/muslimstats.html

Bible translation statistics:
- www.wycliffe.ca/resources/HTML/language_statistics.html

❧ COLUMN 12 ❧
WHAT CAPTIVATES CLOBBERS WHAT IS COMMON

A few years ago, a five-year-old boy named Prince fell down a freshly drilled, eighteen-metre irrigation shaft in India. As soldiers dug a tunnel from an abandoned well nearby, a television camera, lowered into the pit, captured haunting images of the child crying helplessly in the dark, six stories below ground.*

Prime Minister Manmohan Singh was so moved by the boy's ordeal that he was quoted as "praying for Prince's speedy rescue and good health." He also promised to pay for the boy's medical needs. The complex operation gripped the attention of millions, who watched live TV broadcasts that sparked prayers in churches, mosques and temples across the country.

Finally, after a 50-hour ordeal, a soldier, carrying little Prince on his back, emerged from the ground. He was greeted by cheers from thousands of people on the site, while millions of television viewers in India rejoiced at his rescue from certain death.

While Prince waited for his rescuers, elsewhere in India and around the world 39,000 children his age and under died of preventable or easily treatable diseases. Thirteen children die needlessly every minute around the world (four of them in India**), but, in contrast with the situation of little Prince, few people seem to care.

This highlights a problem with human thinking, decision making and action: It's what grips our emotion that gets our attention.

Christians are not immune to this problem. What are the things that move us to pay attention, to give, to pray and to act? Vivid pictures. Dramatic events. That which catches our emotions and imaginations gets our action, our prayers and our money. What is common and routine does not.

Fifty years ago, Jo and I were stirred by stories about Stone Age people groups in South America—the Neglected Continent. Their languages were unknown and had never been written. Their physical, educational and spiritual needs were immense. No wonder our hearts were touched by their plight. No wonder we studied linguistics, cultural anthropology, literacy and Bible translation. No wonder we gladly went to Brazil.

And no wonder we were shocked and dismayed to hear Wycliffe leaders in Brazil tell us, "No, you can't go to a people group yet. Essential support positions must be filled first."

Instead of learning an unwritten language and translating the Bible into it, I managed a mission business office in Rio de Janeiro. Instead of teaching a people group to read, Jo managed a mission guesthouse.

Recruiters had focused mainly on the dramatic—the emotionally high-impact stories of missionaries making first contact with indigenous peoples. Those who responded were potential translators like Jo and me.

Meanwhile, recruiters had given little emphasis to the need for people to do the mundane jobs, the ordinary tasks that support the linguists/translators. Finally, 20 support people—secretaries, teachers, mechanics, carpenters and administrators—arrived in Brazil. Their arrival immediately released Jo and me, and a dozen other translators who had been filling those jobs, to go to the waiting people groups.

Since then, much has changed in the world of cross-cultural missions: use of high technology, ease of travel, partnership with educated nationals, strategic alliances with other organizations, and focus on restricted-access countries. In most mission agencies, however, there is still no change in the need for skilled people to do ordinary, but essential, jobs.

Wycliffe alone has several thousand positions open in nearly 200 job categories. Only a few dozen of these categories have to do directly with linguistics, literacy or Bible translation. Well over 150 categories are of relatively ordinary jobs. Ordinary, but as essential to Bible translators as bakers and cooks are to hungry soldiers on the front line.

Churches need to discipline themselves to make thoughtful decisions, allocating people, prayer and funds to strategically important aspects of cross-cultural missions.

If churches meet only needs that have an emotional impact, they are like the Indian army, labouring for 50 hours to save little Prince, while in that same country, during those same 50 hours, 12,000 other children died needlessly from preventable diseases.

As Jesus said, "You should have practiced the latter, without neglecting the former" (Matthew 23:23, NIV).

*"India rejoices at child's rescue." MSNBC. 23 July, 2006.
  http://www.msnbc.msn.com/id/14001445/.

**"Ashling O'Connor in Bombay." *The Times*. 24 July, 2006.
  http://www.timesonline.co.uk/tol/news/world/asia/article691771.ece.

→ Column 13 ←
What the Recruiter Didn't Tell Me

"Wow, this is cheap!" I said to myself as I started to pump gas into my pickup truck. Gasoline at the Sandy Lake village store is usually much more expensive than at the discount stations in town, but this time it was a bargain.

Then I saw the little note taped to the pump. "Sorry. Pump can't count beyond 99 cents per litre. Price will be doubled at the cash register."

Whoops! I guess I won't fill up after all—just enough to get me to town!

Sometimes things look very attractive at first, but reveal a nasty surprise later on. When I was in high school, all of us desperately wanted our own cars. One friend had enough money, and so he bought himself a car. To pay for the insurance and the registration, though, and sometimes for gas and oil, too, he had to borrow money from his dad. And after a summer of tire-squealing, jackrabbit take-offs from traffic lights, the car needed tires and a new battery to prepare for winter. In the end—surprise! The car owned him.

Another example: A young couple saw a house they could buy with monthly mortgage payments that were no more than the price of the rent they were paying for their apartment. Sounded good. After discussing the idea with their parents, they looked at the cost of lights, heat, water, sewer, garbage, insurance, furniture, lawn care equipment, paint and repairs. They thought about how out-of-town friends and relatives would feel free to drop in, and expect to stay for a couple of days in the extra bedroom. They realised that when they left their apartment to go on an extended trip, they could just lock the door and walk away. But they would need to find someone to look after a house. They stopped to consider the hidden costs.

Missionaries are not exempt from dealing with this hidden-costs scenario. I remember grinding along one day in four-wheel-drive and in low gear through sand, mud and thick bush on the last 70 kilometres of trail into the Canela village. Suddenly the truck was stuck. I got out and saw the left rear wheel, along with the axle, sticking out well beyond the fender. Obviously there was a broken bearing, and I had no spare.

The truck was loaded with valuable goods, food, equipment and work documents. Jo and I couldn't leave it sitting there unguarded. Nor could we wait for someone to come by to help: The only traffic on that trail was occasional mounted cowboys or farmers on donkeys. After prayer, I left Jo to guard the truck.

As I walked six hours back to town, I thought, "Hmm, I don't remember hearing about this kind of situation at that missionary meeting when they called for volunteers and I raised my hand." Hidden, unexpected costs.

It wasn't the first time I had made that observation. Well before the end of our first term, the Brazil field director told us, "Your financial support is so low that you have been borrowing money from other missionaries just to buy groceries. I can't let you stay on the field for a full four years. You need to go home now, and don't come back until you have paid them back and your financial support is up to the required level."

Neither Jo nor I had ever in our lives been in debt. We felt terrible! We had expected that once we left for Brazil, our friends and supporting churches would send in enough money for us to live on, but we suffered an unexpected and disagreeable surprise.

Then there was the time when I had to treat two of my family members with the dreaded 30 days of injections into belly fat to combat rabies. I'm sure no recruiter ever mentioned rabid dog bites.

Probably the worst hidden cost case came in our third term, when a Brazilian government policy expelled all religious workers from Brazilian indigenous villages. We desperately wanted to live and work with the Canelas. The Canelas very much wanted us to live with them in the village. But high-level bureaucracy prevailed—for five years.

The bumper sticker on our little motor home reads, "My Boss is a Jewish Carpenter." The neat part is that to Him there is nothing unexpected—no surprises, no hidden costs. Our Boss knew what lay ahead for the Popjes family when Jo and I raised our hands at that missionary meeting. He knew about the broken truck, the poverty, the rabid dogs and the setbacks.

That is why we can continue to trust Him even as our bodies get older and less dependable. He just needs raised hands. He will take care of the surprises and hidden costs.

Even double-the-price gasoline.

✦ Column 14 ✦
Skinny Pancakes—
The Love Story

Skinny pancakes. That's what we've always called them at our house. Elsewhere these delicacies are known as crepes—those thin French pancakes that lend themselves to a huge variety of fillings, from smoked salmon and bacon to jams and jellies (not to mention whipped cream!). The favourite in our house is simply butter and sugar. Roll it up and yum-mmm.

I consider skinny pancakes the ultimate breakfast. Or lunch. Or dinner. The 100 percent meal.

In the last ten years, however, skinny pancake eating has improved to 120 percent. How? My wife has been warming our plates. Verrrry nice! Now those thin wonders don't lose their heat to cold plates.

What brought on this welcome innovation, after 45 years of marriage? In a word—grandchildren. Nothing is too good for our 8 grandkids, ages 8 to 17.

"World's Greatest Grandma," says the license plate on the front of Jo's car. She lives up to it. Even to the point of pre-warming their plates for skinny pancakes.

"Where's Grandma?" are the first words out of the mouth of our youngest grandchild, when I open the door to let him in. The answer comes from somewhere behind me, "I'm right here, love. Come here."

He is not the only one who's Grandma-focused. I hear these lines from all of them all the time:

"Grandma, I fell and skinned my knee."

"Grandma, I'm sorry. I spilled my milk."

"Look what I found, Grandma."

"I drew this picture for you, Grandma."

"Grandma, my crayon broke."

"Let me carry that for you, Grandma."

"I can drive you there, Grandma—I have a license."

A veritable love-feast. She loved them all before they were born. She loves them, they love her, and the result is that she can't do enough for them, nor they for her. Besides hugs and smiles, both sides invent new ways of showing how much they love each other.

This is Holy Week, Good Friday, Easter Sunday—a remembrance of the greatest demonstration of love this world has ever seen.

To God, nothing is too good for any of the 6.5 billion creatures on earth today. "God so loved the world that He gave his one and only Son…" (John 3:16, NIV). "God is love" (1 John 4:8, NIV). God lives up to His reputation.

A veritable love-feast. He loved us all before we were born. "This is love: not that we loved God, but that he loved us and sent his Son as an atoning sacrifice for our sins" (1 John 4:10, NIV).

He focuses His love on us. And He wants us to focus our love on Him. The first thought when we wake up should be, "Where's God?"

And the answer? "I'm right here, love. Come here."

Then, all day long:

"God, I got hurt. I feel bad."

"I'm sorry, God. I did it again."

"Look what I found, God."

"I wrote this column for you, God."

"God, my computer broke down again."

"God, please use me in Your service."

People who have never tasted skinny pancakes from warmed plates have my pity. But people who don't know that their Creator loves them are infinitely worse off.

Hundreds of millions don't even have God's Easter love story translated into the languages they speak.

My heart breaks for them.

→ COLUMN 15 ←
SACRIFICING OUR MOST VALUABLE COMMODITY

My wife and I drove through an older section of the city of Edmonton this week, passing hundreds of family homes built by the grandparents of today's adults. We both kept saying, "Look how small those houses are!" They were no bigger than the garages for the "starter homes" in the new subdivisions on the edge of the city.

Compared to the economic situation here 75 years ago, people in North America are very well off. Compared to incomes in developing countries today, we're rich—wages here are better, and opportunities to start businesses and make a good living abound.

Even before the current Alberta oil boom, many citizens were living in an affluent society. Large family incomes, costly homes, multiple vehicles, and expensive toys for both adults and children are common in the suburbs and the downtown condos. Acquiring enough money for basic living expenses such as food, clothing, shelter, health and education is no problem for most people. It is true that in many families both spouses work at a paying job to finance what their parents and grandparents would have called "major luxuries."

Money, therefore, is not a scarce commodity. But time is. We may have 10 or 20 times as much buying power as our grandparents, but there is one thing that we have no more of than our ancestors. We have 168 hours in our week, and so did they.

Life today, however, is packed with multiple options—activities our grandparents never dreamt of. These things compete for our time.

Much money and little time explains why many people would rather donate $1,000 to a mission, church or charity than commit to volunteer their service for a few hours a week for three months.

It may also explain George Barna's survey report on traditional church attendance.* He found that millions of North American adult Christians rarely attend church. Most of them, however, do read the Bible and pray regularly, both privately and in a family setting. They come together in small groups to study the Bible. Many tithe their income to parachurch organizations. And a significant percentage have conversations with friends who hold them accountable to live up to biblical principles.

So why don't these Christ followers attend regular church services? Is it because church is not what it used to be? Has the reverence and quiet that goes with an encounter with God disappeared from today's "seeker sensitive" services? That may be the reason for some skipping church. But there may be other reasons.

Maybe one underlying factor is that giving time to attend church is too great a sacrifice. Taking two or three hours to dress, travel to church, attend the service and return home may not be worth the time and bother to some Christians.

It may be that they feel they have more personally satisfying things to do on Sunday mornings. Many earnest Christians come together as close friends, challenging each other, helping each other, teaching each other, and holding each other accountable. To many young people, this is a vastly more satisfying way to spend Sunday morning than simply sitting in a pew as spectators, with hundreds of others.

Churches are starting to adapt. Some hold Saturday evening services, which are duplicates of the Sunday morning service, so people can "go to the lake" on Sunday. Some even offer Monday night "make-up" services, for those who were gone the whole weekend.

Many of us tend to see ourselves as consumers, even in the area of churchgoing. We shop around to find a church that satisfies us. And we leave to look for another one if it no longer meets our needs.

But is meeting our own needs the only reason for going to church?

Is it not also to present ourselves before God, as an act of service to Him?

Isn't that why it is called a church *service*? Yes, He may bless us as we sing, pray and listen to His Word, along with other believers, but is that all?

Going to church with a worshipful attitude, and investing our scarce time, may well be a sacrifice that pleases Him more than the money we happen to drop into the collection plate.

God ordered the Jews in the Old Testament to pick the best lamb from their flock to sacrifice to Him as an act of worship. Do we today need to learn to worship by giving God our most precious gift—our time?

We need to worship God not just by giving financial gifts, but also by giving our time to attend church, and serve in church, in missions and in the community throughout the week.

Our grandparents did not have as much money to spend as we have, but they knew how to spend their time wisely. That is something we can learn from them.

*Barna, George. "House church involvement is growing." Report. 19 June, 2006. http://www.barna.org/FlexPage.aspx?Page=BarnaUpdateNarrow&BarnaUpdateID=241.

→ COLUMN 16 ←
WESTERN CULTURE'S
INDIVIDUALISM REFLECTS SATAN

Arguments and hostilities between cultures are to be expected in Canada—a country trying to live as a multicultural society.

A group of Sikh immigrants from the Punjab region of India, now living in Vancouver, are facing hostile opposition from local long-term Canadian residents.*

This is not surprising given the huge difference between cultural backgrounds. Our Canadian culture was strongly influenced by the teachings of the Bible, not those of Guru Granth Sahib. But there is a twist to this story.

The Sikh families build large multifamily homes. The grandparents, several sets of parents, and their children all live together in the same house. A mutually supportive community is highly valued among the Sikhs. They are suffering hostile criticism by owners of smaller, single-family homes in the area who want to preserve their independent, isolated lifestyle, surrounded by others who value the low-density, single-family home neighbourhood.

Living in an interdependent community like the Sikhs do, however, is far closer to Christian teaching about helping one another than the independent, individualistic way we tend to live in our traditional Canadian culture.

Canada's First Nations people also value a biblical community lifestyle, both in the past and today. Traditionally, most groups lived a clan-based hunting, fishing and gathering lifestyle where each person and family depended on the other.

Several generations ago, government programs relocated entire people groups to reserves and towns to facilitate school and medical assistance. Although the intentions were positive, these moves caused huge cultural upheavals. Some groups totally lost their normal way of life and became economically dependent on government subsidies.

The cultural clash between Canada's individual-oriented government programs and community-oriented First Nations groups continues. Government financial help, training and other assistance is generally made available, not to communities, but to individuals, furthering their independence from the First Nations community. In spite of this, even among those who live in large cities, interdependent community living is still valued among First Nations people.

Cultures and lifestyles of every people group on earth have both positive and negative aspects. Unfortunately, North American culture admires the rugged pioneer. We rank independence and self-reliance highly and dislike depending on someone else. This self-centred drive, which favours the free action of individuals, is a strong value in our country and in many of the western nations. But it is wholly unbiblical. "I can do it by myself, I don't need you," is okay coming from a two-year-old learning to put on his shoes, but it is not the way God designed people to live.

God made us in His image. And He is not an individual. God is a community—Father, Son and Holy Spirit. Each member of the Holy Trinity relates to the other on an equal basis. God made human beings in this same pattern and image, to relate to each member of the Trinity and to each other.

Human beings of whatever racial, ethnic or national background, who live in close relationship with each other, reflect the Holy Trinity.

North American self-reliant, self-indulgent individualism reflects the self-centredness of Satan. As C. S. Lewis so aptly put it, "To admire Satan, then, is to give one's vote…for a world of…incessant autobiography."**

God's will for human beings today is to live in community with each other. He calls this the Church. The Christian Church is a group of unique individuals, each one equal before God, but who are in an interdependent relationship with one another. Saint Paul uses the metaphor of a human body to describe how closely Christians in the Church are dependent on each other. Each body part differs from the other, yet is essential to the total body. So each Christian differs from every other Christian, yet is essential for the Church to function as a living organism.

It is impossible to live a well-rounded Christian life marooned alone on a desert island, or in an individualistic society. Check out the more than 40 statements from the mouth of Jesus and the pen of Saint Paul, each one using the term *each other* and *one another*, preceded by verbs such as *love*, *forgive*, *help*, *bear burdens* and *pray*.

God calls His people to demonstrate to the world how to live in caring relationship to each other. We cannot do that if we insist on conforming ourselves to our independence-loving western culture.

No national culture on earth is perfect. Not Sikh culture. Not the traditions of First Nations. Not western culture and lifestyles. That is why God's "Instructions for Living" must be translated into the mother tongue of every ethnic society on earth. When people groups learn what God's design and intention is for human relationships, they have the tools to judge their own culture, and the option to act counter-culturally—like salmon swimming against the current.

Simply having God's "Instructions for Living" translated into our own language and printed in a nicely bound book is no guarantee that our lifestyle will change. Western societies are the proof.

We need to read God's Word, soak our minds and hearts in it, and then commit ourselves to live accordingly. To do that, we need the help of others.

That is how He designed us.

---

*"House size limit provokes angry reaction." *CBC News OnLine*. 6 December, 2006. http://www.cbc.ca/canada/british-columbia/story/2006/12/06/bc-surrey-homes.html.

**Lewis, C. S. "A preface to 'Paradise Lost.'" *The Quotable Lewis*. Ed. Wayne Martindale and Jerry Root. Wheaton: Tyndale House, 1990, 528.

→ COLUMN 17 ←
THE ESSENTIAL TOOL NOT EVEN GOD CAN DO WITHOUT

"Your permission to live and work in the indigenous village is hereby cancelled."

Jo and I, along with all other missionaries working with indigenous peoples in Brazil, received that message from the Brazilian government about ten years after we had begun to work with the Canela people. They begged us to stay, and we tearfully explained that we wanted to stay, but that we were guests in Brazil, so we had to obey our hosts.

Jo and I left our village home, returned to our house at the missions centre in Belem, and prayed. We waited for things to change. We got involved in other aspects of missionary ministry, but as the months turned into years, our hearts longed to return to the Canelas.

One Friday afternoon, someone knocked on the door of our house. When I opened it, I was dumbfounded to see Jaco, our very best Canela translation associate. I had not seen him for three years, and now here he was, 800 kilometres from his village.

"Jaco, how did you get here?" I asked, welcoming him in.

"I walked for two days. Then I caught a ride on top of a rice truck for two days. Then I rode on a bus all day. And then I walked some more. Now here I am for a good, long visit, and what's to eat?"

We sat him down and fed him over and over again that weekend, as we listened to his travel adventures and the news from the village. His visit was off to a great start.

On Monday I asked him, "How about doing some more translation?"

He said "Yes," so we sat down at the translation table. I dusted off the books I hadn't used in years, and said, "Let's pray." I prayed, in the Canela language, thanking God for bringing Jaco to us. I asked God to bless our translation work. To close my prayer, I said, "Hamre," meaning *Amen*, and opened my eyes.

I was about to start talking when I noticed Jaco still had his eyes closed. Then he started to pray: "Hello, Great Father in the Sky. This is me. My name is Jaco. You might remember me, since I am one of those in the village who just recently began to follow."

That's when I began to cry. I had never heard a Canela pray. After 13 years of learning, working, praying and waiting, this was the first time I knew there was a Canela Christian. I could hardly wait for him to say h*amre*, so I could ask him, "How did this happen?"

"Do you remember those carbon copies of Luke and Acts you sent into the village? One afternoon I was in my hammock reading them when I suddenly asked myself, 'Jaco, how much longer are you going to just read these papers? When will you start to obey them?' I answered myself: 'I will obey right now.'

"I went outside and looked up into the sky and said, 'Great Father in the Sky, according to what I read in these papers, you are very good and I am very bad. Please do something for me.'"

Then Jaco asked me, "And do you know what the Great Father did?"

"No, what?"

"He adopted me into His family," Jaco said, using the same expression that the Canelas used when they adopted Jo and me into Canela families and we became fully functioning members of our new families and of the Canela culture.

Jaco went on. "Then I went out and talked with many of my friends, and now a whole group of us is following the Great Father in the Sky, according to the words on the papers."

Although for three years there had been no missionary, no preacher and no evangelist in the Canela village, God's Spirit had been at work. He has worked in Canela society for centuries. More than once, He has kept them from being massacred. He has shaped their culture and language, even developing the powerful practice of adoption—a perfect metaphor for what He wanted to do for repentant Canelas.

But if He was at work all those centuries, why didn't He bring the Canelas to repentance and adoption long ago?

He could not, or perhaps He would not. He was missing an essential tool. But as soon as that tool arrived, in the form of first-draft, hard-to-read carbon copies of Luke and Acts in the Canelas' heart language, He grabbed the tool and used it to bring Jaco and other Canelas to Himself.

The Holy Spirit now has a 750-page book of clear, well-translated Scriptures in Canela to use to bring dead Canela souls to life and grow them into people filled with Himself.

In thousands of people groups around the world, however, God's Spirit is working, and waiting—still waiting—for that essential tool to be translated into their heart languages.

In Praise of Single Women Missionaries

"We believe you would be a superb missionary, and we would be happy to send you out to represent our denomination on the mission field in Nigeria, except for two things: You are a woman, and you are not married."

Johanna Veenstra, a godly and capable young woman who passionately loved her Lord and wanted to build His Kingdom in the needy places of the world, was disappointed at the board's decision.

Fortunately for her, and for the Kingdom of God, a number of individuals in her local church sponsored her ministry privately. They prayed. They sent funds. They encouraged her during her 14 years of ministry in Nigeria. Seven years after her death on the field, the churches she planted continued to grow in strength and number, and the mission board formally took on Nigeria as one of their mission fields.

The history of worldwide missions is replete with stories of how God used single women in astonishing ways to build His Kingdom. Gladys Aylward, for instance, evangelized in China and cared for hundreds of orphans before and during the Second World War. A book, entitled *The Small Woman*, was written about her. It was also made into a movie, *The Inn of the Sixth Happiness*.

A generation before her, Mary Slessor lived and worked in Africa. Her story is the subject of two books, one of which is titled *The White Queen of the Calabar*. She astounded Christians back home with matter-of-fact accounts of her death-defying dealings with indigenous peoples.

Jo and I hold single women missionaries in high respect. I remember with joy the gifted single women, though relatively anonymous, who helped us succeed in our linguistic and translation work. We could not have done it without them.

Patricia, a translator in a related language, calmed our fears that we had made a mistake in identifying 17 phonemic vowels in the Canela language—there seemed to be way too many. She explained that the language she worked with had 16. She helped us to write up a clear description of the Canela sound system.

Eunice patiently walked me through the process of sorting out and writing down all the knowledge of the Canela grammar system I had in my head, to make it accessible to others.

Margery, after completing her own translation project, painstakingly checked our work and happily reported that she had not found a single collocational clash in Acts. That was 25 ago, and although I have now forgotten what a collocational clash is, at the time I was enormously encouraged to hear that we did not have any.

Gloria poured into us her knowledge and experience of developing learn-to-read booklets that practically taught themselves.

Isobel's enthusiasm and encouragement helped us to produce a series of booklets that prepared oral learners to read the Scriptures.

Ruth's commitment to "her" people, and her willingness to live with them for months out in the bush without even a hut to call home, rebuked my love of comfort and challenged me to greater sacrifice.

Jane doubled my effectiveness when I suddenly found myself in a major administrative position. She knew where to get the information I needed to make good decisions. She knew everything and everyone, and had the experience I lacked.

The life of a single woman in a foreign land and culture is not easy. Indigenous societies often do not know how to treat single women. As well, many young women would like to marry and have a family. Yet although they know that it is highly unlikely that they will find a suitable marriage partner on the mission field, they go, impelled by love of God and His Kingdom.

I praise these single women. So does God.

Johanna Veenstra

Veenstra, Johanna. *Pioneering for Christ in the Sudan*. Grand Rapids, MI: Smitter, 1926.

Beets, Henry. *Johanna of Nigeria*. Grand Rapids, MI: Grand Rapids Printing Co., 1937.

Palmer, Timothy. *The Reformed and Presbyterian Faith: A View from Nigeria*. Bukuru: TCNN Publications, 1996.

Gladys Aylward

Burgess, Alan. *The Small Woman*. New York: Buccaneer, 1959.

Aylward, Gladys, and Christine Hunter. *The Little Woman*. Chicago: Moody Bible Institute, 1970.

The Inn of the Sixth Happiness. 1958. http://www.imdb.com/title/tt0051776/.

Mary Slessor

Bueltmann, A. J. *White Queen of the Cannibals: The Story of Mary Slessor of Calabar*. Charleston, SC: BiblioBazaar, 2006.

Evans, A. R. *Mary Slessor : The White Queen of Calabar*. London: Oliphants, 1962.

⊹ COLUMN 19 ⊰
THE CASE OF THE MISPREPARED TEACHER

In the fall of 1994, Laurie Gough completed her formal training in First Nations education, stepped into her first classroom, and had the shock of her life.*

The group of third graders in Kashechewan, a small Cree village on James Bay in Ontario, ignored her totally and did as they pleased.

What pleased them was punching, shouting, screaming and throwing dead mice and birds at each other. They tore down the classroom curtains to make a hammock, and ripped up books or scribbled in them. In the chaos, they also managed to cut off their teacher's braid, throwing it at her from across the room.

"It never got better," she writes. She left at Christmas, a physical and emotional wreck.

Laurie Gough was fully prepared academically, but was utterly unprepared for the realities of dealing with children in a tiny village far out in the bush.

Not only was she unprepared, she was misprepared.

Her head was full of ideas about Canada's First Nations people that simply were not true—at least in her particular situation and at that time. She described herself as a "bright-eyed idealist, yearning to live in a tepee and voice the virtues of native culture."

Instead she went into severe culture shock when neither the children, nor their parents, nor the community's elders behaved anywhere near what she had been led to expect.

Truth is the best preparation. But Laurie was not told the truth. She even thought all indigenous peoples would be avid environmentalists, while in that village they were anything but.

Had she been able to spend some time with a teacher who had taught in that school, she would have had a chance to adjust her expectations to that particular situation. But she hadn't.

I remember when Jo and I moved into the Canela village in Brazil, with our three little preschool daughters. Were we idealistic? Yes! Were we trained academically? Yes!

But we also had many long talks with other linguist-translators who were living in similar situations. These talks flushed out any fantasy ideas and preconceived notions we might have had, replacing them with a solid layer of truth.

It was this preparation that moved us to develop solid relationships with the chief and the elders—relationships that lasted until we left, 22 years later, after completing the project. Right from the beginning, the chief told us he wanted his people to learn to read, first in their own language and then in the national language.

We taught adults, not children, because the elders had pointed out, "When the boys go through their puberty rites, they leave behind all the things of childhood. We don't want reading and writing to be a children's activity, to be left behind. Education needs to be an adult thing."

I empathize with Miss Gough. Even though Jo and I were much better prepared than she was, we too battled culture stress while living among the Canela. The stress grew more intense as the months went by. After five or six months of isolation from friends, coupled with zero privacy, our every action noticed, scrutinized and commented upon, we were ready for a break, even though we were well prepared.

Excellent missions organizations lay a solid foundation of truth in academics, as well as in vision and dreams. They make sure that people who have personally "been there and done that" teach their orientation and training courses. Trainees are constantly exposed to field workers fresh from their assignments, ready to share stories of what can happen and how to handle it.

Take Wycliffe, for instance. They have more than 6,000 workers, and most of them partner with thousands of local national workers—tens of thousands of stories! What a resource pool!

During the decades my wife and I were translating the Bible with the Canelas, new linguistic, literacy and Bible translation programs were starting around the world at a rate of about one every two weeks. But now the pace at which new programs begin has increased dramatically to one every three or four days.

The goal of Wycliffe and its partners is to see that every language group on earth that needs it will either have the Scriptures in their language, or have an active Bible translation program in progress, by 2025.

I can hardly wait for the time when well-prepared, well-oriented teams start a translation project for a new people group every day!

*"Laurie Gough." *National Post.* 19 November, 2005. http://www.canada.com/national/nationalpost/news/story.html?id=3bece811-e8fb-4b90-aa15-e8640b2942fe&p=1.

→ COLUMN 20 ←
MOTHERS BUY A BETTER FUTURE

"You don't know who this is, do you?" Don't you hate that question?

The Canela mother sitting on the front porch of our village house asked me again, "Don't you know who this is?" pointing at the smiling young woman sitting next to her, who, bare from the waist up, nursed her baby.

"Of course I do," I said, guessing bravely, "she is your daughter."

She laughed and said, "I have many daughters. You just don't remember, do you? Without your help when she was born, we both would have died."

Then it all came back. We had just arrived in the Canela village. It was our first major medical case—an anaemic young woman having her first baby with long labour and tearing birth, while weak with postpartum fever, and finally producing a sickly-looking child. I gave the mother a shot of antibiotics and some vitamin pills. My wife and I prayed for both of them, and treated them day after day until they were well. And then, more than 20 years later, there they sat on our porch, a happy mother and grandmother.

What's more, both women were there to recite the Bible passages they had memorized, thus earning the right to have a Canela partial Bible of their own when it finally arrived from the publishers.

Mothers pay a painful price to bring their babies into the world. Good mothers continue to pay a price to buy a better future for their children.

My mother left a stable environment, a comfortable home in the Netherlands, and her friends and relatives to immigrate to Canada to buy her children a better future. My mother paid the price of loneliness, living in isolated farmhouses—the only shelter our family could afford. She paid the price of poverty, as we struggled through those first years of immigrant life. My mom kept paying the price to buy us a better future. But it didn't stop there.

Sixteen years later, my mom—now a grandmother—took a deep breath and again paid a painful price to buy a better future. She paid the price of parting. She sent us off to Brazil: I, her oldest son; Jo, her only daughter-in-law; and Valorie, Leanne and baby Cheryl, her only grandchildren. She paid that price to buy a better future, not for herself, not for us, not for her grandchildren, but for the Canelas, a people group she had never met.

Jo's mother paid the same painful price. She bought a better future for the Canelas by sending her only child, her only son-in-law, and the only grandchildren she would ever have. It was nearly four years before either of our moms saw their grandchildren again.

More than 20 years later, both our moms came to Brazil to celebrate the dedication and distribution of the Canela partial Bible. Both of them tasted a little of the reward that awaited them in Heaven. They bought a better future for the Canelas by raising their children as missionaries, and then saying goodbye to them.

When a mother holds her newborn baby in her arms for the first time, the joy is so great it almost makes her forget the painful price. So it was for our moms, who sat on the village plaza and watched the Canela people hug their new Bibles, and heard them sing about God. They said, "It was hard to send our children to be missionaries. Our hearts ached for them. But it was worth it. Oh yes, it was worth it."

⟡ COLUMN 21 ⟡
WE CAN'T ALL BE FOREIGN MISSIONARIES, BUT…

Four of our friends are deeply involved in evangelizing the world and discipling the nations. And no, they are not cross-cultural foreign missionaries! Here's how they did it:

Computer Guy

As a computer technician, his wife and their family of teenage children sat down for lunch one Sunday, they discussed what they had heard a missionary speaker say in church. It was not the first time they had talked about missions, and explored ways in which they could make an impact for God around the world, but this time it was different. By the time the table was cleared, they had made a decision.

Within a month, they sold the house in which the children had grown up, and moved into a much smaller one in a "cheaper" part of town. They gave the difference in the price of the two houses to fund cross-cultural foreign missions.

Farmer

An older couple sold their farm and moved into the city, where the husband started part-time work as an investment consultant. His business associates had large homes backing onto a popular golf course, and recommended several houses in the area to him. He tried living there for a while, but then sold the house and rented a nice, small apartment within walking distance of church and shopping. He shocked his associates even more when he quit his job and started working full time as a volunteer investment consultant at the nearby headquarters of a cross-cultural mission agency. He feels very relaxed and fulfilled, but has yet to hit a golf ball.

Engineer

An engineer negotiated a leave of absence from his job and, at his own expense, moved to Brazil with his wife and two young daughters. After working for several years in maintenance and construction at a missions centre, and having depleted their savings, they returned home and he went back to work.

A few years later, he was offered a major promotion—one that would double his salary and more than make up for the money he had spent during his years overseas. He refused the promotion, since it meant moving to a different city. He felt that his high-school-age daughters now needed the stability of their home, church and school before they left for college. He did not change his mind, even when his boss told him he would not be offered this promotion again. One of his daughters is now a career missionary.

Teacher

While talking about cross-cultural foreign missions, a schoolteacher with a family of three teenagers came up with a plan to take on a major part of the financial support of a missionary. First he led his family through their house and collected hundreds of items for a major yard sale, the proceeds of which went to their missionary.

Next they deliberately "downsized" their recreation, entertainment and lifestyle. They went from skiing to skating; from restaurant dinners to park picnics; from buying books and videos to borrowing them from the library; from movies in a theatre to watching rented videos; from driving cars everywhere to walking and riding bikes as much as possible; and from buying all their clothes new to buying some clothes secondhand. They also practiced my mother's immigrant philosophy, "Wear it out, use it up, make it do, do without."

They sent all the money saved to their missionary friend. Eventually they moved into a much less affluent neighbourhood to minister personally to the immigrants who lived there.

Four families, four stories, but there are tens of thousands of Christians who see themselves as managers of God's money, and who financially support missionaries from their family budget. People like the young working family who gave us $40,000 in 7 years; the carpenter who, during his career, gave $25,000; the businessman who gave $35,000 in the last 30 years; the truck driver family that supported us with $1,000 a year for 44 years; and the single lady hospital worker who drives an old car, but who has given us $50 every month for 600 consecutive months!

These friends could have bought nicer vehicles and fancy furniture, or gone on expensive vacations, but instead they invested in missions, and in so doing, laid up treasures in Heaven.

Jo and I have 6,000 Wycliffe missionary colleagues. Every one of them has dozens of stories like this to tell about friends of theirs.

It may be that tens of thousands of stories will go untold, and the people who are making these sacrifices will live unknown and without praise or reward.

But not forever. God is keeping record. The writer of Hebrews echoes the teachings of Jesus, who often urged people to do good in secret so that His Father could reward them openly: "God is not unjust; he will not forget your work and the love you have shown him as you have helped his people and continue to help them" (Hebrews 6:10, NIV).

→ COLUMN 22 ←
AN UNLIKELY ENCOURAGER

It was more than a rumour, and after two bleak years of yearning, it was our first ray of hope in a sombre situation.

Some years before, Brazilian government officials had refused to renew permits for missions agencies to work in indigenous villages. As a result, Jo and I could no longer teach our Canela friends to read, nor could we study linguistics and translate the Scripture with them. But now, finally, we had permission to make a brief visit to the Canela village! We had written authorization from the head of the government Indian agency in the capital, Brasilia.

We asked our colleagues at the translation centre to pray, packed up our four-wheel-drive truck, and drove for two days to get to the local government office responsible for the Canela village. We waited two more prayer-filled days until the government official returned from a trip, so we could present our authorization and pick up the key for the padlocked gates at the edge of the Canela reservation.

The next morning, cheerful and full of hope, I walked into the government office and gave my authorization document to the official. He was a man whom I knew quite well from years of reporting to him about our work. Once I had even pulled his jeep out of a mud hole. He glanced over the document and brusquely handed it back to me.

When I asked about the key, he refused to give it to me. No *ifs*, *buts*, or *maybes*. It had something to do with internal politics, and his refusal was final.

"What's more," he assured me bluntly, "I dislike foreign missionaries, and I hate you bringing a foreign religion into an indigenous village." With that, he ordered me out of his office.

I was devastated. I stumbled out of the building, crossed the sidewalk and slumped down on the curb, feet in the gutter, face on my knees and shoulders heaving with great, racking sobs. I cried like a lost child.

Suddenly a strong arm hugged me around my shoulders, as someone sat down beside me on the curb. I felt a beard rubbing the side of my head. Then an Italian-accented voice whispered in my ear in Portuguese, "Cheer up, my son. God is greater than the government—much greater."

Through my tears I saw God's angel of encouragement, wearing the flowing beige-brown robes of a Franciscan priest.

Many years later, I told this story as an illustration of encouragement. Afterwards, a man strongly criticised me. "You are a wimp and a weakling!" he said. "You should have told that Roman Catholic priest he was on his way to Hell."

I knew how my critic felt.

I grew up in Hilversum, Holland, in the shadow of the towering Saint Vitus Cathedral, in a neighbourhood called Little Rome. Our family was the only Protestant one on the block.

Since my father was a fish butcher, each Friday I had the hateful job of delivering parcels of fish to the convent that was part of the cathedral. Shivers ran through my ten-year-old frame each time I saw the stern, unsmiling visage of the nun glowering at me through the bars of the receiving wicket, in the outer vestibule. The long walk down the cold, echoing, stone-floored hall to the door of the convent filled me with dread. I never knew which massive door might open suddenly to reveal a robed priest glaring down at the little Protestant boy who dared to walk those sacred halls. I knew that if it happened, I would have nightmares for a week.

I had paid close attention in school during history lessons, where I heard story after story of Dutch Protestants burned alive for owning a Bible in their own language, their children tied in sacks and thrown into the canal to drown. On a school field trip, the teacher had pointed out the "drowning spot" in that canal. True, all these things happened long ago, but who knows when they might start doing it again. "Roman Catholics hate you, so stay away from them," sounded like sensible theology to me.

But sitting on that curb, 30 years later, being hugged by that priest, I had changed my theology. Many other things had changed too. No one had yet said, "I'm sorry, we were wrong," but actions speak louder than words. The centuries-old Roman Catholic hostility for ordinary people having God's Word in their own language was disappearing in many countries. Now Roman Catholic scholars were translating the Word of God into languages of people groups all over the world. I had met some priests and nuns who were involved in Bible translation in Brazil.

When, after five years of "exile," government policy changed and we were finally able to return to the Canela village, we translated not just the New Testament, but also a representative portion of every book of the Old Testament. The 30 Psalms we chose to translate included those used in the Roman Catholic Mass.

The first time Bible portions were read by Canelas at a public ceremony, attended by the entire village, was during the once-a-year mass officiated by my encourager, the Franciscan priest. It was the first time the Canelas had a chance to understand the meaning of this significant ritual.

Years later, when the Canelas received the Word of God in a partial Bible, newly published in their own language, many of them followed its light on their path to the Living Word, and trusted in Him to save them.

I sometimes wonder if that would have happened if God had not sent His beige-robed, bearded encourager to me at the right time.

IT'S OKAY TO BE RICH

Many Christians have an unbiblical bias against rich people as a group.

I know a businessman whom God has blessed with an almost unbelievable talent for recognizing and making good business deals. Being a devout Christian, he is also incredibly generous. It seems that the more money he gives away, the more God helps him to create wealth. He and his family live out in the country and his wife is constantly on the go in her volunteer ministry, even over icy winter roads. So he bought her a high-quality imported vehicle she could depend on. Would you believe that a Christian leader criticized her for driving an expensive car?

This leader is not the only Christian who feels that having wealth and enjoying some of it is wrong. Since we live in a materialistic society obsessed with money and the consumption of goods, the Church's teaching on material wealth needs to be crystal clear. Unfortunately it is not. As a result, many Christians don't know how to think biblically about creating and spending wealth.

We have all heard good sermons on how God hates those who become rich by stealing, or by dealing dishonestly in business, or by exploiting the poor. We also know that the Bible warns rich people, even rich Christians, who trust in their wealth instead of trusting in Him, or who hoard their wealth instead of sharing it with those in need.

There is, however, another side to the teaching about wealth that we don't hear as often. It is both clear and simple.

For starters, God loves rich and poor alike. He loves skilled musicians, as well as those who can't carry a tune in a bucket. In the same way, He loves those to whom He has given the ability to generate wealth, and He loves those who could not recognize a good business deal if it was handed to them on a platter.

The Bible also teaches clearly that God, as Creator of everything, owns it all. There is not a single coin in the world on which Jesus cannot put His finger and proclaim, "This is mine." According to Deuteronomy 8:18, God is the source of all wealth. The verse says, "Remember the Lord your God, for it is He Who gives you power to get wealth" (Amplified Bible).

God delights in those who use the abilities He has given them to create wealth honestly and see themselves as managers of His money, not owners.

Although a musician is talented, she still needs to work long and hard to develop her talent. In the same way, those to whom God has given the talent to create wealth still need to sacrifice personal pleasure, and discipline themselves, to become highly proficient in their business. They need to take risks, to work hard, and to use the talents God gave them. When such people continue to trust God, hold their accumulating wealth loosely, and share it with those in need, God is pleased.

If a gifted musician refuses to work hard to develop her talent, and holds back from using it to serve God, we lament the loss to God's Kingdom. In the same way, if a businessman refuses to use his God-given abilities to create wealth, and is thus unable to meet basic human needs, we shake our heads and wonder what is the matter with him.

God does not distribute His talents evenly. Not everyone can be highly successful financially, in the same way that not everyone can be a concert pianist.

So back to the story of the rich Christian who bought his wife an expensive car. Can he use some of the wealth he created to do nice things for himself and his family, as long as he generously funds God's work around the world and shares with those in need?

The answer is the same as for this question: Can a musician and her family personally enjoy the music she creates, as long as she is generous in playing for others so that they can enjoy it too?

The answers are based on the biblical principle in 1 Timothy 6:17, which teaches the wealthy to have the right attitude about their wealth, and ends with, "…God, who richly provides us with everything for our enjoyment" (NIV).

Saint Paul repeats the ancient biblical principle of Deuteronomy 25:4, on personally enjoying the fruits of our work, in his instructions to Timothy in 1 Timothy 5:18, writing, "Thou shalt not muzzle the ox that threadth out the corn…. The labourer is worthy of his reward" (KJV). And in 2 Timothy 2:6, he writes, "The hardworking farmer should be the first to receive a share of the crops" (NIV).

Owning, using and enjoying top-of-the-line equipment, vehicles and homes is the privilege of those whom God has given the ability to buy such things. With this privilege also comes the responsibility to use wealth wisely, furthering God's work around the world and showing love to those who are in need.

Some of you may be saying, "I am not wealthy, so none of this applies to me." Note that if you own the computer on which you are reading this email, you are in the same economic bracket as the world's wealthiest 10 percent. Nine out of ten people are poorer than you—over five and a half billion of them.

UNSPOKEN AND UNINTENDED MESSAGES FROM FATHERS

"Little pots have big ears and small potatoes have big eyes." This Dutch saying warns parents to be cautious of how they act and what they talk about when their children can see and hear them.

As a child I had big ears and eyes. I was only 12 years old, but I knew that things were not going well for my father's retail fish business. He worked at least 14 hours a day, 6 days a week, in his fish shop next to our house. He was doing three times the business he had been doing before the Second World War, but was still sliding into bankruptcy. The problem, my big ears told me, was taxes.

Holland was overcrowded, and the economy was stagnant. To solve these problems, the government made it easy for unemployables, such as farm workers and other unskilled labourers, to leave the country. Tens of thousands left each year. In 1949, my uncle, a farm labourer from Friesland, left for Canada, with his family, under this program.

With the Dutch government's "Bigger Is Better" policy, there was no future for small businesses in the Netherlands, so Dad decided to follow my uncle to Canada to buy a better future for his five kids. Since employers and taxpayers like my dad were not eligible for financial help to emigrate, he began to sell everything he owned— vehicle, equipment, business and home—to buy one-way boat tickets to Canada.

At lunch one day, the phone in the hall rang, and my dad left to answer it. He returned a few minutes later, his face white and drawn, mouth pinched, eyes burning with anger. He turned to my mom. "They found more taxes we need to pay. But they won't let us sell the house until we have paid all the taxes." Suddenly he ran from the dining room. I could hear him retching in the bathroom.

That week, Dad sold nearly all the furniture, borrowed money from the bank, and paid the taxes. He eventually sold the house, paid back the bank, and finally got an exit visa. Then he borrowed money from a brother to pay for the tickets. We boarded the immigrant ship, *Volendam*, in the late afternoon, six days later.

As the ship headed out into the sea, Dad and I stood at the stern, looking back. He gripped the railing with both hands, staring beyond the white wake to the low black shoreline as it receded into the twilight.

The bell rang for dinner. He didn't move. I looked up at his face. It was tight and angry, his eyes glaring at the land of his birth, where he had lived for 40 years—his childhood in his father's home, with 8 brothers and sisters, his marriage and his own children, the war with its daily escape from death, his 28 years of hard work since the age of 12. But now he was leaving it all. He owned nothing but the clothes on his back and a few bits of furniture he had built himself. His own country had sucked out his lifeblood.

As the last black strip disappeared under the horizon, he cleared his throat and spat in disgust at his native country. Then he took a deep breath of clean, fresh, salty air, and said, *"En nu naar Canada"*: "And now to Canada." He took my hand and we walked briskly to the dining room.

Fifteen years later, Dad and Mom began to make trips to the Netherlands to visit relatives. I did not. I did not return to the land of my birth for 45 years, and then only because it happened to be on the way to a Wycliffe conference in Germany.

I doubt my dad intended to pass on to me his anger and disgust for the Netherlands, but he did. We never talked about it, but the unspoken message stuck.

In our churches, it is not just from the pulpit that messages are preached. Spiritual fathers in church constantly pass on messages and attitudes to children and teenagers with "big ears and eyes." The younger people hear, see, remember and adopt these messages and attitudes as their own.

They notice that the only time a missionary comes to speak in the Sunday morning service is when the pastor is away on vacation or at a conference.

They notice that the pastor gets a guaranteed salary, but foreign missionaries have to raise the funds for their salary and ministry. Sometimes this fund-raising takes years.

They notice, when they themselves serve in short-term missions, that at their return from weeks overseas they get a mere five minutes to download their spiritual blessing and excitement to the congregation.

They notice that elders and leaders get much more excited discussing home improvement projects than when planning for a Kingdom-building venture.

These things all say, "Cross-cultural foreign missions is peripheral to the church."

These spiritual fathers do not intend to pass that unbiblical message on to "big eared, big eyed" children in the congregations, but they do.

They never talk with them about these things, but the unspoken message sticks. The next generation perpetuates the attitude.

→ COLUMN 25 ←
BAD DEATH, GOOD RESULT

Thousands of villages dot the West African landscape, each inhabited by one of a huge variety of ethnic minority peoples, each with their own culture and language.

The Anufo* were a strongly traditional group, and quite different from other cultures, especially in their beliefs about the power of malevolent local spirits. Among their many fears was the horror of dying a *bad death*—that is, a death cursed by the spirits. To die simply of old age or of a common sickness, surrounded by family and friends, was a good death. To die by violence, with blood and disfigurement, was a bad death. All who lived in Anufo villages believed this.

In terror of the spirits, the Anufo would have nothing to do with the corpse of a person who had died a bad death. No matter how much the deceased person had been loved and respected in life, he or she did not receive any normal funeral performed by relatives. Instead, the village shaman—the spirit medium—would braid a piece of rope, loop it around the ankles of the corpse, and drag it far out into the bush. There he would abandon it, rope and all, to rot and be eaten by the hyenas and vultures.

The Gospel of Mark was translated into the Anufo language, and the good news about Jesus spread throughout their villages. A few people responded to God's message and became followers of Jesus Christ. But most of the Anufo strongly resisted the idea of leaving their ancestral ways of placating the spirits around them. They were too afraid of the spirits to even listen to the Christ followers tell about Jesus.

One day, a tremendous tropical lightning storm swept through one of the villages. As all those outside ran for shelter, lightning struck a man, killing him instantly. He was one of the few followers of Jesus.

After the storm was over, the villagers gathered round to look at the charred corpse lying on the rain-soaked ground. This was a very, very bad death!

The Christians arrived, knelt around the dead man, and began to prepare his body for a proper burial. When the shaman walked up with his piece of rope, he was aghast, as were the rest of the people. They crowded closer, loudly insisting that the shaman be allowed to drag the bad death corpse away.

"Don't mess with that bad death. If you do, our crops will fail, our wells will go dry, and our children will get sick and die!"

At that, one of the Christian leaders stood up and asked the shaman to wait a few moments. He walked to his hut and returned with a newly translated copy of the Gospel of Mark in his hand.

"Let me explain why we are not afraid of the spirits," he said.

Then, as the villagers stood quietly to hear the explanation for this astounding precedent, he told them the story of God's Son Jesus, His life, and His death—His incredibly bad death. He described the excruciating scourging, the bloody torture of the crown of thorns, and the hours of agony while dying on the cross. It was a far worse bad death than any of them could have imagined. Then the Christian leader told them about the resurrection and the plan of salvation, showing them that Jesus' bad death opened the way to God and eternal life.

"God used the extremely bad death of His own Son to produce very good results. Therefore, He can do the same for any of us. The only bad death any of us must fear is to die without having a relationship with God."

Then, while the entire village watched, the believers finished preparing their brother's body, and buried him in the village cemetery. There, in the hearing of many of the villagers, they prayed for God's great Spirit to protect them from vengeful evil spirits.

In the weeks that followed, no wells went dry, no crops failed, and nothing worse than usual happened. This event made such an impact on the villagers that many eventually came to know God. They then spread the good news about Jesus' power over the local spirits to other villages.

One man suffered death. His wife lost her husband, and his children, their dad. The whole village suffered loss. But that was only part of the story. God used that death and pain as one part of a much greater story—one that brought life and joy to a whole people group.

For those of us who suffer today, may David's testimony in Psalm 30:11–12 someday be ours:

"You turned my wailing into dancing;
you removed my sackcloth and clothed me with joy,
that my heart may sing to you and not be silent…" (NIV).

*Anufo (as they call themselves), or Chokosi (as they are called by outsiders), live in the northeast part of Ghana. The New Testament translation into Anufo is now complete and the dedication celebration was held in February 2007.

FOOLING OURSELVES: TAP, TAP, TAP

I own and use a high-technology pedometer—a birthday gift from my oldest daughter and her family. It has missiological ramifications.

"Walk more; eat less!" says my doctor. That should be enough to motivate me, but it isn't. I need help. That's where my pedometer comes in.

Talk about bells and whistles! It records my every step and uploads the information to my computer, which calls up a website and draws a graph of my day's walking. It also displays a bar graph for the past seven days. A red line shows my week's personal average, and a yellow line the average of others of my age and weight class. It also tells me how far I've walked, and how many calories I've burned. It's hi-tech motivation, and it works!

Even though I am the only one who sees these motivating graphs, the thought came to me one day that I could easily make my graphs look even more impressive, without having to walk any more than I already do. I could increase my daily step record by tapping the pedometer rhythmically on my thigh, while lounging in a lawn chair enjoying a double scoop ice cream cone. It would be a great way to fool myself.

Hi-tech, pedometer-equipped walkers are not the only people in danger of fooling themselves. Churches are too.

Although numerous North American churches are far more proactive in cross-cultural ministry than they used to be, many more churches are fooling themselves. Some churches believe they are vitally interested in cross-cultural missions, but they are really just tapping their pedometers against their thighs.

For instance:

Church #1—A large world map hangs in the foyer with pictures of missionaries they partially support all around it. Several missions slogans surround the map. Nearly 100 families attend this church, yet the total amount given to all those missionaries combined is less than half the salary of the youth pastor. Tap, tap, tap.

Church #2—This church has the word *missionary* in its name, but neither the current pastor nor the previous two pastors have ever traveled to Asia, Africa or South America to visit a cross-cultural mission field. The pastor never preaches on cross-cultural missions, and the church hears missionary speakers only when he is away on vacation. Tap, tap, tap.

Church #3—Many large photographs of missionaries this church has been supporting partially for the past several decades are hung in a conspicuous place. The missionaries and their projects receive significant amounts of money from this church every year. So far so good. But only five percent of the congregation gives to the missions budget. The other 95 percent of the congregation gives only trace amounts to missions. Tap, tap, tap.

Church #4—For many years, the women's mission circle has prayed for missionaries. Individuals in the congregation continue to financially support various missionaries. The church has an impressive overall strategic plan for church growth and ministry. However, it has no slot for a missions coordinator, nor a plan to replace current missions supporters when they die or move away. The church's strategic plan for growth makes no mention of cross-cultural missions. Tap, tap, tap.

Church #5—Most members of the large youth group go to Latin America for a month each summer to work in orphanages, build homes for the poor, or do child evangelism. The entire missions budget is spent on supporting these short-term summer missions. The church supports no career missionaries. Tap, tap, tap.

Jesus gave the responsibility of evangelizing the world and discipling the nations to the whole Church. The whole Church certainly includes several thousand missionaries engaged in cross-cultural missions. But even more importantly, from the aspect of "going, giving and praying," Jesus gave the Great Commission to hundreds of millions of believers gathering in a million local churches all around the world.

Cross-cultural missions must be the central focus of ministry for everyone—not just for missionaries and their leaders in missions agencies, but also for Christians and their pastors in local churches everywhere.

Those churches that consider themselves active in missions because of their name, their history, or some relatively peripheral missions activity may look good, but they are only fooling themselves. Tap, tap, tap.

I need to put another 5,000 steps on my pedometer right now. Forget about the ice cream cone.

→ COLUMN 27 ←
TAKING ON THE UNITED NATIONS

Many a bet has been settled in beer bars and liquor lounges by referring to the Guinness Book of World Records. (No, I'm not drawing on personal experience—I saw it on TV!)

Since the Guinness book is so valuable for resolving arguments, you'd assume that its researchers would follow the ancient wisdom of the journalism adage, "When gathering facts, make sure they are." Turns out that is an unwarranted assumption.

Take, for instance, the area of translation. Here is what I read on the United Nations website of the Office of the High Commissioner for Human Rights (2006).*

"The Office of the High Commissioner for Human Rights has been awarded the Guinness World Record for having collected, translated and disseminated the Universal Declaration of Human Rights into more than 300 languages and dialects: from Abkhaz to Zulu. The Universal Declaration is thus the document most translated—indeed, the most 'universal'—in the world."**

What? Only 300 languages? And Guinness accepted that as a world record?

Let's see. When the UN was founded in 1945, a Bible, a New Testament or some substantial amount of Scripture had already been translated into about 1,000 languages. Including the preamble, the 30 articles of the Universal Declaration have 1,773 words in English. That's nearly the same length as Jesus' speech on how people should relate to God and each other, in Matthew 5 and 6, or about two and a half pages of the 747-page Canela partial Bible, which my wife and I translated.

In comparison, during the past 58 years, this very brief UN document was translated into 321 languages.*** During the same

58 years, full Bibles, New Testaments, or whole books were translated into 1,700 languages.****

This discrepancy stirred me up, so I wrote to Mary Robinson, the UN High Commissioner for Human Rights:

Subject: UDHR most translated document? Not quite.

High Commissioner for Human Rights

Dear Ms. Robinson,

You have a right to be pleased and excited to see the UDHR being translated into so many of the world's languages and dialects. Your enthusiasm, however, may have gotten the best of your office when it published these paragraphs on your website.

The UDHR being translated into 300 languages is impressive, but the full Bible has been translated into 422 languages, and the full New Testament of the Bible into a further 1,079 languages. 876 other languages have at least one book of the Bible translated into them.

That totals 2,377 languages that have at least some major portion of the Bible translated into them. Besides that, a further 1,640 languages have Bible translation projects going on in them right now. You could check it out on this website: http://www.wycliffe.ca/resources/HTML/language_statistics.html.

What interests me, as a Bible translator for the Ramkokamekra-Canela people of northeast Brazil, is that the concepts and principles of the Universal Declaration of Human Rights are found in, and based on, the rights stated so clearly in the Bible. So, in a way, we Bible translators are doing our part in helping to lay a foundation for your excellent work around the world.

Sincerely,

Jack D. Popjes

A substantial portion of the Bible will be translated and disseminated into every one of the world's 6,900-plus languages long before the United Nations' Universal Declaration of Human Rights manages the same feat.

The Guinness Book of World Records notwithstanding, you won't go wrong to bet on that.

P.S. I never received any acknowledgment from Ms. Robinson, but I did notice that the Guinness World Records webpage stating the UN claim has been removed.

*Universal Declaration of Human Rights. http://www.un.org/Overview/rights.html.

**"The Universal Declaration of Human Rights is the most universal document in the world." http://www.unhchr.ch/udhr/miscinfo/record.htm.

***World Language Statistics and Facts. http://www.vistawide.com/languages/language_statistics.htm.

****Wycliffe Bible Translators of Canada: Statistics. http://www.wycliffe.ca/resources/HTML/language_statistics.html.

→ COLUMN 28 ←
CONTEMPT FOR A HOLY BOOK

Each day, as my family and I visited the little one-room house with the hole in the seat, we used a page of an old Eaton's catalogue in lieu of toilet paper. This showed no disrespect for the Eaton's company or for its products; it was just common money-saving practice in rural Canada during the 1950s.

I remembered those years while reading newspaper accounts of military prison guards being accused of tearing pages out of Islam's holy book, the Koran, and flushing them down the toilet. Disrespecting the Koran was a highly effective way of showing contempt for Muslim prisoners and their religion.

The Koran* is the focal point of all Islam. It is held as the uncreated word of God, written on golden tablets in Paradise. For Muslims today, the Koran is both a physical proof for, and the sound of, Islam. Reciting the Koran in Arabic creates a sacred and spiritually powerful moment. Muslims believe the Koran can never be correctly translated into any other language, because Arabic is the holy language. True believers read the Koran aloud in Arabic.

No wonder, therefore, Muslims around the world were appalled and infuriated when stories of such a gross desecration of the Koran began to spread.

Although we, as Christians, believe the Bible to be the Word of God, we do not consider the Hebrew and Greek languages in which it was written to be holy. In contrast to Islam, Christianity is a religion that depends on translation of the Bible. No true believer needs to learn Hebrew, Greek or even Latin in order to recite the Bible and create a holy moment. Instead, God's Holy Spirit speaks through the translated Scriptures, revealing God to the hearts of people. What's more, only where the Bible has been translated into the heart language of the people has Christianity flourished.

Although Christians do not consider a copy of the Bible to be holy in the same way that Muslims consider the Koran holy, we do respect the physical book. I recently realized this anew during an intensive inspection of my carry-on luggage at an airport in the U.S.

The white-gloved inspector repacked my case, placing my Sunday shoes on top of my brown leather Bible. As I reached in to change the arrangement, he angrily told me to keep my hands out of my case. So I asked him to move the Bible, wrap it in a T-shirt, and put it in last, on top of all the contents. He did so, giving me a look that said, "Weirdo religious fundamentalist fanatic!"

Some people have no problem with putting their shoes on top of their Bible. I can't even put my Bible on the floor. Maybe that is going overboard. Never mind. What bothers me more is the disrespect many Christians show the Bible by going day after day without reading it. We may read it as a habit, or as liturgy, but our minds and hearts are disconnected from one another. That is major disrespect.

Others read it, and even think about it, but do not obey it. That is like reading a love letter from your friend, wherein he or she asks you to do something, and then ignoring it. That is neither an act of love nor respect.

Individual Christians are not the only ones who disrespect God's Word. The Church, as a whole, does too. Now, 2,000 years after the Bible was written, over a quarter of the world's languages still have no translation of even a single verse of God's Word. Although the Church around the world has benefited from having the Scriptures in the heart languages of the people in its pews, it still has not passed God's Word on to everyone. There are still hundreds of millions of people speaking thousands of languages, in continents such as Africa and Asia, in which not one verse of the Bible has yet been translated.** That is the greatest disrespect.

No Christian would dream of using a page of the Bible as toilet paper. Yet statistics show that the Church as a whole puts a very low priority on Bible translation.

That, too, is holding the sacred Word of God in contempt.

* "Introduction to the Koran." *Encyclopedia of the Orient*. http://i-cias.com/e.o/index.htm.

**Gordon, Raymond G., Jr., ed. *Ethnologue: Languages of the World*. Fifteenth edition. Dallas: SIL International, 2005. Online version: http://www.ethnologue.com/.

THIRST

So what's the big deal about a couple million people in and around Vancouver having to boil their drinking water for a few weeks?*

Heavier than usual autumn rains washed soil and silt into the water reservoirs, muddying the water well above acceptable levels. So what?

Compared to over a billion people in Asia and Africa who never, ever have clean, safe water to drink, Vancouver's temporary muddy water problem is a very small Canadian drop in a very large world bucket of water problems.

Okay, I admit it. It is a big deal to us Canadians who have grown up with sparkling clean drinking water pouring out of our taps every day of our lives. We take clean water for granted and don't even miss it "until the well goes dry," as the saying goes. But let's put this in perspective. The tap water in parts of Vancouver looks a bit grey, but it is safe to drink. One thousand separate tests for bacteria came back negative. Try that with the unboiled, unfiltered water in the drinking cups of hundreds of millions of people who live along rivers like the Ganges, Amazon, Niger, Nile and Yangtze.

My wife and I know what it is like to boil drinking water. We spent most of our child-raising years in a small indigenous village in the Brazilian bush. We boiled water every day, in a 12-litre aluminum pan, on a homemade, clay, wood-burning stove. We were lucky. It was a solvable problem. The creek had plenty of water, the bush had plenty of firewood, and after we got the routine set up, we had plenty of time. Boil the water, pour it into a large clay pot to cool, and then into the clay dispenser pot with the little plastic tap on the bottom. No big deal, as long as you didn't mind drinking lukewarm, smoky-tasting water. We didn't mind. It was a small price to pay for better health. We did it for decades.

We easily provided clean water for our family, and the situation in Vancouver will soon be just a memory. But around the world, unsafe drinking water is still a major problem crying out for a solution.

Dr. Lee Jong-wook, former director-general of the World Health Organization, put it clearly: "Once we can secure access to clean water and to adequate sanitation facilities for all people, irrespective of the difference in their living conditions, a huge battle against all kinds of diseases will be won."***

Drinking dirty, unsafe water causes all kinds of diseases. Nearly 90 percent of diarrhoeal diseases are caused by unsafe water supplies, which lead to inadequate sanitation and hygiene. As a result, 1.6 million children under five years of age die every year from cholera and other diarrhoeal diseases.** Three little kids died from these causes since you started reading this column.

So, when clean drinking water once again starts to flow from Vancouver taps, will people just say, "Whew, I'm glad that's over!" and go back to life as usual? Or will they find some way to help the rest of the world get clean drinking water?

It is not hard to get involved. The World Wide Web lists dozens of nonprofit organizations that focus on drilling wells or setting up water purification plants in needy areas of the world. Nearly all Christian mission agencies working in countries plagued by poor water supplies have departments that help bring clean water to needy people. They already have the infrastructure and the know-how. What they do not have is the money.

Because of the Vancouver crisis, people across Canada are more aware of the importance of clean water. Now here's hoping they will provide funds for organizations that are meeting the needs of a thirsty world.

Jesus told the story of the future final judgement in which the King will praise his people and say, "…I was thirsty and you gave me something to drink." The people will respond, "Lord, when did we see you…thirsty and give you something to drink?" The King will reply, "…Whatever you did for the least of these brothers of mine, you did for me" (Matthew 25:35, 37, 40, NIV).

The old prophet Amos also presents a strong picture of worldwide thirst, not for clean drinking water, but for the words of God (Amos 8:11). One out of five people in the world do not have access to clean drinking water. That is serious.

What is also serious is the fact that speakers of two out of five languages do not have access to the Word of God in their mother tongues. Many of these minority people groups suffer both physical and spiritual thirst.

Now that is a big deal! It doesn't hit the TV news, but it is a major concern for God.

It should be a major concern for His people.

*"Greater Vancouver boil-water advisory lifted." *CBC News OnLine*. 27 November, 2006. http://www.cbc.ca/canada/british-columbia/story/2006/11/27/bc-boil-water.html?ref=rss.

**"Water, sanitation and health links to health." *World Health Organisation*. http://www.who.int/water_sanitation_health/publications/facts2004/en/.

→ COLUMN 30 ←
IT'S TO DIE FOR

He was finally hanged in prison, in Singapore. Nguyen Tuong Van was guilty of drug smuggling, no doubt about that. The packets of heroin, enough for 2,600 hits, were found taped to his body. That the penalty for smuggling was death was also clear. No doubt he recognized, too late, that 400 grams of heroin were not worth dying for.*

But some things are definitely worth dying for. Like following Jesus, although it is not preached much these days.

What we tend to hear in North American churches is, "God gives us the privilege of living for Him, and making Him famous through our work and life."

What we do not often hear is, "God sometimes gives us the privilege of dying for Him, making Him famous through our suffering and death."

No wonder much of the world is turned off by North American Christianity. It seems like an insipid, bland, dull, flat and weak religion.

Quite a contrast to Islam. At a Wycliffe Canada annual meeting, missiologist T. V. Thomas reported that "an internal Islamic document states that within six months of the spectacular September 11, 2001, attack on America, 42,000 white Americans became Muslims because Islam was seen as a faith worth dying for."** Every Iraqi and Palestinian suicide bomber reinforces that view.

What made the four Christian peacemakers taken hostage in Iraq a few years ago so unique was their willingness to risk their lives. Jim Loney, Harmeet Sooden, Norman Kember, and Tom Fox deliberately put themselves into a dangerous situation, not for personal gain, but to follow the command of Christ to work for peace.

After three months of captivity, Tom Fox was killed by sword-wielding terrorists who were blinded by a version of Islam that preaches hate, and deafened to everything except violence. The other three men were freed a month later. As Christians and members of Christian Peacemakers Teams, they believe that making peace is a goal worth risking their lives.***

Fifty years ago, in Ecuador, five young missionaries were killed by spear-wielding Waodani tribesmen blinded by fear and deaf to everything except killing. (The local Quichua called the Waodani Auca, meaning *savage*.) Jim Elliot, Nate Saint, Ed McCully, Pete Fleming and Roger Youderian believed that making contact with this violent people group to bring God's message of peace was worth risking their lives.****

That bloody event had a powerful impact on millions of Christians around the world. Christianity was seen as a religion worth dying for. In the following decade, thousands of young people, including my wife and me, confirmed that we were ready to risk our lives to bring the message of peace to every people group on earth.

Since the Church in North America needs help to focus on the Christian's duty to suffer and die, if need be, it is appropriate that this 50-year-old story has been retold. *End of the Spear,* a powerful feature film, reintroduces this headline-making event to the world. It also reminds the Church that Christianity is a faith worth dying for.*****

Christianity, as practiced outside of North America, leaves no doubt in peoples' minds that Jesus is worth living and dying for. Our daughter and son-in-law visited one village in India where the home of every Christian family had been burned to the ground the previous year. The Christian church where they met had been burned down and rebuilt three times. The Church just keeps growing.

We western Christians have many physical and material resources for spreading God's Kingdom. Our brothers and sisters in Asia and Africa, however, have something we lack: a well-developed, biblically sound theology of suffering.

What will it take for us North American Christians to learn that some things are to die for?

---

*"Appeals fail to save Australian." *CBC OnLine News.* 1 December, 2005.
  http://www.cbc.ca/story/world/national/2005/12/01/nguyen051201.html.

**Thomas, T. V. "Devotional." Wycliffe Canada Annual Meeting. 1 December, 2005.

***"Hostage release bittersweet." BBC News. 23 March, 2006.
  http://news.bbc.co.uk/2/hi/middle_east/4837632.stm.

****Elliot, Elisabeth. *Through Gates of Splendor*. Wheaton, IL: Living Books, 1981.

*****End of the Spear. 2005. http://www.imdb.com/title/tt0399862/.

SHORT-TERM MISSIONS: MUST DOS FOR SUCCESS

I had my first missions experience among First Nations people in Whitehorse and Ross River, Yukon, while working as a short-term missionary (STM) for seven months in the late 1950s. During the sixties, seventies and eighties, I experienced the opposite end of short-term missions as I received STMs and worked with them in Brazil. Finally, during the '90s, and in the past few years, my experience was as a recruiter and sender of STMs from Canada and the Caribbean.

I suffered from mistakes made by others, and for some I made myself. Brooding over the resulting failures moved me to compile a list of "must dos" that I wish I had read long ago!

Character, Competence, Compatibility, Calling: The STM must be a solid, growing Christian, know how to do something useful, be able to get along with the rest of the group, have a spiritual calling or motivation strong enough to bear up under inconvenience, and be prepared to make some personal sacrifices.

Preparation: The sending group, church or school must brief the STM about the travel, the living accommodations, the food, the schedule, the work expected, the attitude needed, and above all, about the culture of the people he or she will be serving. This may take many hours, over several weeks, before the trip.

Expectations: The sending group, the receiving organization, and the STMs must all share their expectations with each other clearly, and through negotiation make sure the planned experiences will match at least some of the expectations of each. The agreed-upon expectations should be written down clearly, and each of the three groups should have a copy.

Safety and Security: STMs must learn to take care of their cash, passport, belongings and personal safety. Travelling outside of North America demands far more vigilance in these areas than what they are used to at home. A crisis management plan needs to be in place to deal with medical or security emergencies in the host country.

Debriefing: The STM must know from the start that there will be an in-depth debriefing while still in the host country, with a written evaluation of the experience, and an outline of the next steps that need to be taken by the STM. Based on the responses, it may be valuable to have one or more follow-up meetings after the STM returns home. Sharing with the sending church, school or prayer group needs to be done within seven days, at most. After that, the vision fades.

Cultural Experience: The sending organization must take into account the level of cultural experience with which each STM is able to cope. Some first-timers need to start at an entry level experience, working as part of a team with people of a different culture within one's own country and language. An advanced experience would be living alone in a foreign country, not knowing much of the language, while boarding in the home of a national family. Dozens of various situations separate those two cultural extremes.

Leadership: The receiving organization must have excellent on-site leadership. Cross-cultural, multi-lingual project management is far more difficult than regular, home country management.

Ministry Partners: Each STM must not only have sufficient financial backing, but also some ministry partners back home committed to praying specifically for the STM. The prayer partners can pray for health, safety and for a good time, but mostly they need to pray for long-lasting spiritual results, both in the life of the STM and as a result of his or her ministry.

What Next?: After the first short-term missions experience, each STM must plan what to do next. Each subsequent experience should be more challenging to the STM than the previous one. It could be at a higher cultural level, or with greater leadership responsibilities, a wider ministry, or even a career in missions. Older folks might like to simply repeat the same trip, with the same experience and the same ministry, but for younger people, this might be seen as a waste of the STMs' time and their partners' money.

Benefit: One benefit of short-term missions is, of course, the ministry performed by the STM. But the main benefit may well be the impact of the experience on him or her. Veteran career missionaries need to see the STM team not as cheap workers, but as potential recruits to the world of missions.

Each year, thousands of people enjoy positive, life-changing, successful experiences in short-term missions. They have more missions interest, pray more, give more and often plan to get involved again at a higher level.

I have asked hundreds of my missionary friends and colleagues what was the main influence in their decision to become missionaries. Almost without exception, they mentioned a successful short-term, cross-cultural missions experience.

These successful experiences did not just happen. They came as a result of following a carefully considered list of "must dos."

→ COLUMN 32 ←
BETTER THAN AN ENAMEL PLATE

I will never forget that girl's prayer during night class!

We were in the last stages of the Canela translation program. Two dozen young Canela men and women surrounded me, sitting on logs, heads bowed in prayer. We had sung hymns set to Canela indigenous music patterns, and in a few minutes would read and talk about a new draft of the translated Scriptures.

Now it was time to pray. I heard prayers asking God to heal sick children, for a good crop, and for help to find a lost bush knife.

Then a young mother prayed:

"Great Father in the Sky," she began, "I want to thank You for sending our brother Prejaka, and our sister Tehtikwyj, to us so long ago when I was just a little girl. They taught us to read our own language. Then they worked with us to translate Your Words into it. Now we can read Your Letter to us. Now we are discovering that You love us very much. Now we can learn how we can live to please you. Please help them to finish the Book soon."

Then came the part that brought tears to my eyes and engraved itself into my memory.

"I also want to thank You for all Prejaka and Tehti's friends in Canada. Every month their friends send money to them. They know that our brother and sister don't have a food garden here like we do. They need money to buy food, and their friends in Canada send it to them.

"They don't send it just because they are their friends. They send it because they are our brothers and sisters. Just as You are our Great Father, You are their Great Father too.

"They could keep the money and buy nice things for themselves. Maybe they see a new enamel plate or a shiny spoon, and ask themselves, 'Should I buy this for my family?' But then, they decide not to buy anything, but to send the money to our brother and sister so they can stay here and help us have Your Word.

"And they sure chose right, because Your Word is so much more valuable than a new spoon, and better than an enamel plate. As a reward, give these friends, our brothers and sisters, lots of healthy children; make their gardens grow well and keep them from getting sick. Amen."

Just think, Bible translation programs are going on in nearly 2,000 languages around the world right now. A hundred programs have been completed in the last few years. It is very likely that while you are reading this column:

Somewhere in the world, people are reading or hearing the Word of God in their own language for the first time.

Somewhere, the Holy Spirit is revealing the Father to someone who has only recently heard about Him.

Somewhere, the Holy Spirit is inspiring new believers not just to thank God for His Word and for those who bring it, but also to ask Him to bless those who send the money which makes it all possible.

Somewhere, God is blessing donors to Bible translation and cross-cultural missions who are responding to prayers by new believers such as that young Canela mother.

Therefore, to those of you who give to Bible translation and cross-cultural missions: Keep it up. Somewhere, someone may be thanking God for you.

Someone whom you will not meet until eternity may be praying God's blessing on you because, as that young Canela mother said,

"You sure chose right."

→ COLUMN 33 ←
FRUSTRATED WITH GOD

Don't you sometimes get ticked off at God? After all, He knows everything, and, if you are a Christian, He lives within you. So why didn't He remind you to (fill in your own frustrating bit of recent forgetfulness here)? Or, as in my case once, something under God's control just wasn't working out the way I had planned.

I was in Calgary, attending Wycliffe Canada's annual general meeting, surrounded by 100 Wycliffe colleagues who were presumably eager to buy multiple copies of my latest book, *A Poke in the Ribs*, but the Wycliffe bookstore had none to sell. They were all stuck somewhere in customs or on some snowbound truck. Frustration!

Sometimes our Friend Within does remind us of things we need to do. At other times He lets us suffer the consequences of our forgetfulness—a hard but good way to learn. Sometimes He allows us to suffer through circumstances over which we have no control. And occasionally He just has a little fun with us.

Take the case of new Wycliffe members Ben and Renee. There they were, fully trained and ready to go to East Africa to serve in a country that desperately needed their skills and ministry. They were praying and searching for both prayer and financial partners to join their support team. They were meeting people and getting ready to travel.

One day, running late, they hurriedly jumped into their car to drive 30 minutes across town to their mom's house for dinner. Ten minutes into the drive, they realized they didn't have the book they had intended to bring with them. After a quick U-turn, they raced back to get it.

"Better call Mom and tell her we'll be late."

"Okay, where's the cell phone?"

"Oh no! I just remembered! I put the book and the cell phone on the roof of the car when I unlocked the car door, and left them there!"

The book and phone naturally had fallen off the roof as they drove away. They looked for them on the way back, hoping to see them on the street, but found nothing.

Frustration! Self-recrimination! "How could I have been so dumb?!"

They turned around again and despondently drove to Mom's house to tell their sad story, explaining why they were so late. They arrived to hear happy news. Someone had picked up both the book and the phone off the street, pushed a few speed dial numbers, and eventually got through to their mother.

After dinner, a much relieved Ben and Renee drove out to pick up their lost phone and book—a book about Christians and money. That's when God started having some fun.

It turned out that the couple who picked up the phone and book were also Christ followers. Ben gave them one of his and Renee's picture prayer cards and told about the ministry they were planning to do in East Africa.

The next day, Ben and Renee got an email message from their new friends, who told them that they were excited about their upcoming ministry and promised them $5,000 towards their travel and start-up needs.

A few months later, Ben phoned them, wondering if they would consider being regular financial partners in their ministry. They immediately offered $300 per month, and haven't missed a month since.

Back to the delayed arrival of the boxes of my books: Was God having some fun with me? Will He turn that frustration into something that will make Him look good? I don't know.

Is God in charge? Does He know what He is doing? Double "Yes!"

Will I stop being frustrated with God, relax, give in and trust Him?

Yes…eventually.

WORST-CASE SCENARIO—ALMOST

"My doom has come upon me!" Hector shouted, as Achilles deflected his last javelin. He knew he was about to be slain.*

I knew exactly what Homer's defenceless warrior felt like, when, after breakfast, I walked into my hotel room in Oceanside, California, and saw the empty spot on the desk. My laptop computer was gone, along with the printer, flash drive, and my leather rolling computer case (Father's Day gift) filled with other peripherals.
Oh yes, and my passport—I had planned to fly back to Canada the next day. And there would be no Look column going out to readers via email on Saturday.

It was a worst-case scenario. Fresh notes and preparations for a dozen speaking engagements in Alberta and British Columbia during the rest of the month had disappeared, along with all our personal records, bank account numbers, credit cards, etc. Yes, they were buried under several layers of passwords, but, as we all know from watching TV crime shows, a computer lab operated by criminals can break into any computer. The dreaded spectre of a stolen identity lurked in the back of my mind.

It was what I had always feared and tried to prepare for. I usually back up my documents and other important data every week, and always the day before I travel, usually on two different media: an external hard drive and a flash drive. I was traveling back to Canada the next day, and had planned to back up my data right after breakfast. Thus that fateful morning the laptop was already hooked up to the external hard drive.

Now here's the good news! Incredibly, although the burglar had grabbed the laptop and the printer, he had disconnected the hard drive I use for backup and left it sitting on the desk. Whew! What a relief!

It reminded me immediately of a saying I heard the other day: "God will not bring any unnecessary tears into our lives."

I also thought of the little motto in my office at home: "Remember that nothing can happen to you today that God and you can't handle."

Both of those sentiments are based on the text I learned the week I became a Christian—1 Corinthians 10:13 (NIV). "No temptation (or trouble) has seized you except what is common to man...." (The investigating police officer told me theft from hotel rooms was common in Oceanside.)

"...And God is faithful; he will not let you be tempted (or afflicted) beyond what you can bear. But when you are tempted (or thrown into trouble), he will also provide a way out so that you can stand up under it."

God knew that if my main backup device had also been stolen, I would not have been able to stand up under it. To lose 1,700 document folders with 50,000 files of stories, messages, linguistics, Canela translation, resources, half-started books, letters, decades of diaries and other keepsakes, etc., was a horror I could not have faced. Even salvaging some of that material from old backup CDs would have been a daunting task. But God is good and He spared me from that. Thank you, Lord.

There is one other thing. All this tends to encourage me to no end. Could it be that Satan, the great enemy of truth, hates my Bible-translation-oriented speaking and writing ministry enough to try to hinder it? "Sweet!" as my grandkids would say.

Another old saying goes, "What doesn't kill you makes you stronger." I feel stronger already.

Jesus kept His promise when He said, "In this godless world you will continue to experience difficulties." He also said, "But take heart! I've conquered the world" (John 16:33, *The Message*).

No doom in that news.

*Homer. *The Iliad*. Trans. Samuel Butler. The Internet Classics Archive. http://classics.mit.edu/Homer/iliad.22.xxii.html.

→ COLUMN 35 ←
MUMBLING ATHEISTS

The interviewer's first question startled me. Although a self-confessed atheist, the host for the national CBC radio program *Trans-Canada Matinee* was obviously enjoying his visit with us in the Canela village. He began the interview with an introduction:

"Tonight, we are located in a small native village in the heart of the Brazilian jungle. The nearest telephone is 400 kilometres away. It took four days to travel the last 75 kilometres into this village. I'm visiting Jack and Jo Popjes and their three preschool daughters, a young family of Canadians who have already lived with the Canela people for a year, and are expecting to spend a good part of their lives here."

Then he turned to me and said, "Jack, you and your family are western Canadians. The Canela people and their culture have survived for hundreds of years in these jungles. What gives you the right to come here from Alberta and change their indigenous culture and way of life?"

What an astonishing question for an atheist to ask a Christian missionary! He obviously assumed we would actually have some effect on the solidly established Canela culture.

I had been expecting a different question. Something like, "What on earth gives you the idea that the two of you can make any kind of difference in a thousand-year-old culture?"

It was such an obvious mismatch. I can see it clearly:

In the far corner! An indigenous way of life, grounded and rooted in a massive oral history and a unique kinship and naming structure, further bolstered with a complex system of festival cycles, songs, dances, ceremonies, customs, puberty rites and rituals, all practiced by villages of hundreds of people living in a culture and way of life that survived centuries of intertribal wars, and that has already withstood decades of contact with the Portuguese-speaking Brazilian over-culture.

And in this corner! A young couple in their late 20s, with three preschool children, still trying to learn the unwritten language, still ignorant of much of the culture, without political connections or influence, near-zero financial and material resources, living like their indigenous neighbours in a mud-walled, palm-thatch shelter, and cooking in an iron pot over an open wood fire.

Clang! The bell rings. Pow! The Canela culture wins by a knockout in the first round.

Well, not quite. That young couple did have something else. They had a Book. A very old Book. A Book written thousands of years ago by people speaking completely different languages, and for people of cultures utterly different from the language and culture of the Canelas. But surely even such a Book would not pose a threat to the entrenched ghost-, demon- and witchcraft-oriented belief system of the Canela people!

The very same God who created the Canelas, however, inspired that Book. He was the One who gave the Canelas their language, and who sought to guide them as they developed their culture. That same God wanted the Canelas to know Him through His message to them in that old Book. That young couple believed that when the Canelas read for themselves about God and His love for them, changes would be as natural as healthy seeds sprouting in warm, damp soil. And a quarter of a century later, that is exactly what has happened.

Isn't it great that God uses us cross-cultural missionaries to give His Word to thousands of people groups around the world? The results are astonishing.

Through His Word in their own language, God becomes more real to indigenous peoples than the spirit beings they have feared. As they personally experience God's love and forgiveness, they are freed to forgive others, stepping out of the endless revenge cycle. In this way, God transforms lives and redeems whole cultures.

When atheists sit quietly by themselves, with no one looking, and honestly study the positive changes the God of the Bible has worked in the lives of people and societies, I wonder if they mumble to themselves,

"Hmm, amazing. If I didn't know any better, I'd say that God was involved."

⊹ COLUMN 36 ⊹
FROM ONE DITCH INTO THE OTHER

Let me put it as gently as I can: Television and organized children's sports are the two greatest family-destroying inventions operating today. I am only partly joking.

Theologian and apologist C. S. Lewis told his readers that Satan always sends errors into the world in pairs—pairs of opposites—so that while avoiding one error, people would fall headlong into the other.* He didn't know it when he wrote it, but it applies 100 percent to what is happening in North America today.

We all know there is nothing wrong with children watching television, in moderation and under parental guidance. But, according to the American Academy of Child & Adolescent Psychiatry, children in North America watch far too much unsupervised television: an average of three hours per day, including weekends and holidays.**

They are influenced by the thousands of commercials they see each year, many of which are for alcohol, junk food and toys. Some shows are filled with violence and sex, and are not meant to be seen by children at all, yet many children watch them, entirely unsupervised—another negative moral impact. Children who watch a lot of television tend to have lower grades in school, read fewer books, and, what many parents feel is even worse, TV-watching kids tend to get fat.

Childhood obesity, Stanford University studies agree, is caused or made worse by children watching too much television, and eating too many high-calorie foods, often while watching TV.***

So, in order to avoid this gross error, millions of parents have opted to climb out of the slimy ditch of unlimited television watching. But instead of leading their children down the narrow road of moderate amounts of parent-supervised TV, interspersed with moderate family exercise, they and their children have plunged headlong into the muddy ditch of organized children's sports. Aaargh!

It is probably impossible to overemphasize the deleterious effects, but I'll try.

Millions of parents all across North America have enrolled their children in hockey, football, soccer, swimming and whatnot. They then spend billions of dollars on sports equipment and gazillions of hours driving their children from one sports practice or game to another.

The television may be off, but there is still no time for families to eat together, talk with one another or play together. Or come to hear a missions speaker at church, I might add (even when I am the speaker!).

Yeah, I admit it—that is what started this tirade. I usually speak about 70 times in 40 or 50 cities each year, and I notice that, except for Sunday mornings, the audiences are mostly college-and-career young people, empty nesters and old folks like Jo and me. Parents with school-age children are mostly absent, busy shuttling their children to the next sports practice.

Speaking of shuttling, the impact on the environment is significant.

Statistics I have recently made up conservatively estimate that the amount of fuel expended by parents driving their children to and from organized sports activities is equivalent to launching a space shuttle every 30 minutes around the clock, every day.

And here's what bothers me the most. Googling *childhood television watching* yields thousands of websites decrying the evils of children watching too much TV. But search for websites about the negative impact of organized kids' sports on families, and all you find are shouts of joy and waving palm branches.

The child psychiatry sites will timidly hold up a tiny red flag and caution parents against assaulting the coach, umpire or referee, but that's about it. There's nothing about the family-destroying dangers of overdoing sports.****

Girls, fortunately, seem to be slightly less affected by sports mania. Dave Barry, my favorite sociologist, points out, "If a woman ball player has to choose between catching a fly ball and saving an infant's life, she will choose to save the infant's life without even considering if there are men on base."

One more thing: As I often say to my son-in-law, who is a preaching pastor, "And you never hear this preached about...."

*Lewis, C. S. *Mere Christianity*. New York: Macmillan, 2001, 156.

**"Children and watching TV." *American Academy of Child & Adolescent Psychiatry*, 54 (2001). http://www.aacap.org/publications/factsfam/tv.htm.

***Robinson, T. N. "Television viewing and childhood obesity." Division of General Pediatrics and Stanford Center for Research in Disease Prevention, Stanford University, Stanford, California, USA. http://www.ncbi.nlm.nih.gov/entrez/query.fcgi?cmd=Retrieve&db=Pub Med&list_uids=11494635&dopt=Abstract.

****"Children and sports." *American Academy of Child & Adolescent Psychiatry*, 61 (2005). http://www.aacap.org/publications/factsfam/sports.htm.

GOD ONLY KNOWS HOW MUCH

Thirty-seven billion dollars sounds like a lot of money. When investor Warren Buffett donated that amount to one of the richest charitable foundations in the world, he doubled its resources. News agencies were all over it.

But it made me wonder, why do they think it is newsworthy?

True, it makes an interesting story. The world's second richest man ($44 billion) gives 80 percent of his fortune to a charitable foundation run by software giant Bill Gates, the world's richest man ($50 billion).*

Bill and his wife Melinda plan to retire from actively making money and, with Warren, switch to spending even more of their fortune to combat disease and ignorance around the world. In 2005, for instance, 70 percent of the grants from the Bill and Melinda Gates Foundation were for traditionally underfunded basic education and health programs (HIV, malaria, tuberculosis) in 100 Third World countries.

As a world Christian, I am, of course, delighted that more money will be spent to address the world's most challenging inequities. But why did it hit the news?

It can't be the amount of money. The $70 billion Gates Foundation plans to spend at least $2 billion a year. But amounts vastly larger than that are already being distributed to money managers to meet the world's multiple needs.

God only knows how much money He has already given to His people to spend in doing His work here on earth. The estimates of the amount of wealth currently in the hands of God's people, His money managers, vary wildly, but dwarf the amount available in the Gates Foundation.

Urbana researchers reported in 2000 that the total yearly income of the world's Christians was about $12 trillion.** A tithe of that would be $1.2 trillion, which God expects His people to spend to meet the spiritual, physical and educational needs of the world each year. If all His people around the world actually gave 10 percent of their yearly income, it would take 600 Gates Foundations to keep up with them.

Here are some staggering statistics about just the accumulated wealth in the hands of Christians in North America. For the sake of round numbers, and to be conservative, let's say that one in ten North Americans is a Christian, and that Christians have about the same income as others.

A 1993 study from Cornell University projected the value of inheritances passing from one generation to another within North America from 1990 to 2040 at $10 trillion.*** At 10 percent, this would be $1 trillion in the hands of elderly North American Christians who need to pass all this money on before they die.

Another study in October 1999, by Boston College, forecasts much higher levels of wealth transfer. They estimate that from 1998 to 2052 (depending on savings rates, national economy, medical costs, etc.), between $41 trillion and $136 trillion will be passed on.

Since we are estimating that 10 percent of the people holding this wealth are Christians, $4 trillion to $14 trillion is being passed on or will need to be passed on before these individuals die during the first half of this century.

My calculator is starting to smoke, but it tells me that over the next 50 years, elderly Christians will need to give away up to $280 billion every year. Even if they gave 90 percent to their kids, and 10 percent to God's work, that yearly $28 billion would be 14 times the amount that the Gates Foundation budgets to distribute.

God only knows how much money He has given to His people to do His work, but the estimates are absolutely staggering.

What is just as staggering is the fact that Christians in North America give only about two percent of their income to God's work. And nearly all of that is spent not out in the desperately needy world, but in their own churches, to meet the needs of people who are already Christians.

That is probably what makes the Buffett donation news. He actually gave away 80 percent of his wealth to benefit the sick, ignorant and poverty-stricken people of the world.

What's more, empty tomb inc. studies show that the more Christians earn, the smaller the percentage they give to God. In the USA in 1933 (the depth of the Great Depression), Protestant church members gave 3.2 percent of their income. In 1955, just after affluence began spreading through North American culture, it was still 3.2 percent. But by 2005, when Americans were over 554 percent richer, after taxes and inflation, than in the Great Depression, church members were giving only 2.6 percent of their incomes to their churches.****

God has given His people the financial power to heal, to educate, to relieve poverty and to bring news of spiritual life to billions of people around the world. Not only do we have the financial power, but we have the spiritual resources as well.

When Christians around the world begin to give to God's work in the way that God intends us to give, billions of dollars will be available to fund His work everywhere on earth. And Christians will hit the news too.

On the other hand, if we just keep on spending God's money on ourselves, how long will it be before He pulls the plug on the funding and fires us?

*"Warren Buffett donates $37 billion to charity." *BBC News OnLine News.* 26 June, 2006. http://news.bbc.co.uk/2/hi/business/5115920.stm.

**The Church Around the World* [video]; *Lost Peoples* [video]; *Poverty* [video]; Madison, WI: Intervarsity/Urbana, 2000.

***Herman, Tracy. "Detecting demand." *Registered Rep: The Source for Investment Professionals.* 1 April, 2000. http://registeredrep.com/mag/finance_detecting_demand/.

****"US per capita/per member giving as % of income" [diagram]. *Giving Research.* http://www.emptytomb.org/fig1_05.html.

⟶ COLUMN 38 ⟵
LOADING THE TEETER-TOTTER

Many young people today talk about getting personally involved in missions, but hesitate to commit themselves. We mission mobilisers may well be to blame. We who are in the business of recruiting people and raising funds for cross-cultural mission work may be focusing on the wrong end of the teeter-totter. No wonder we don't get the results we pray for.

When I join my four California granddaughters on the playground, they like to play with me on the teeter-totter. Two or three of them on one end can't budge me—it takes all four of them, plus a playmate, to lift my end off the ground. I can't make myself lighter, and even when I give myself a little push, the moment my feet leave the ground, down I go again. The only way they can make my end stay up is to load more kids on the other end.

We mission mobilisers are facing a teeter-totter situation just like this. We load up the *value* and *benefit* end of the teeter-totter by telling young people, their parents and potential donors, "The Great Commission applies to you today. You will be so satisfied knowing you are helping to meet the basic physical and spiritual needs of long-neglected people groups. You will be working with other dedicated people." We may even mention some of the side benefits of tax deductions and living in an exotic country.

We then load up the *cost* and *consequences* end of the teeter-totter. "You will need to ask people to pray for you. You will need to raise your own salary and ministry expenses from your friends, relatives and church. You will be lonely in isolated locations. You may be working in a country where the dominant religion is militantly anti-Christian. You donors may need to reduce your personal lifestyle in order to give to missions. You parents won't see your children or grandchildren for years at a time."

Before we even mention tropical illnesses and the difficulty of transportation, the *cost* and *consequence* end of the teeter-totter is as solidly stuck on the ground as if an overweight grandpa were sitting on it.

That's when we make our mistake. We try to lighten the cost end by saying things like, "But you'll get training and help to raise funds. You may even be in a location where you can email your family. You won't be the only ones dealing with these difficulties." But it's useless. They suspect, and we know, that the actual cost will be much greater than they can imagine. Significant giving involves personal sacrifice. Missionaries and their children may even lose their lives overseas.

We need to stop trying to balance the teeter-totter by lightening the cost and consequences end. It is as hopeless as trying to make a grandpa weigh less. Instead we need to load up more value and benefit on the other end. We need to start saying things like, because of your commitment today:

You will someday hear the Lord of the Harvest saying, "Well done, good and faithful servant. Come and share my happiness!"

You will make a significant difference in the world, and you will carry that knowledge and satisfaction with you to your grave and beyond, no matter what else you do with your life.

You will see people from every ethnic group, language and nation standing around God's throne in Heaven, singing His praises for all eternity, and know that God used you to make this happen. You will be overwhelmed with joyfully exuberant greetings from people who are in Heaven because of your ministry.

Your only regret will be that you did not get involved in this ministry sooner.

The cost end of the teeter-totter is temporal, here and now, in this world only. The value end is eternal and heavenly. It's the vision for which Jesus died and rose again.

IF YOU'VE NEVER TRIED MONEY…

After recognizing the value of laughter, bread and wine, King Solomon the Quester said, "But it's money that makes the world go around" (Ecclesiastes 10:19, *The Message*). Money makes missions go around too—and does a lot of other things.

One day my youngest sister, Annie, took her four-year-old son, Roger, and the baby to a park with a waterslide. It looked like fun, and other kids were having a great time, but Roger had not been on a waterslide before and was afraid to try it. Since she couldn't leave the baby to go with him, she kept urging him to try it alone, but he kept on hesitating.

Finally Annie said, "I'll pay you if you try it." That did it. Roger slowly climbed the stairs, and with a look of grim capitalistic determination, he let himself go. A few seconds later, he jumped out of the pool at the bottom of the slide, his face beaming, and ran around to the stairs shouting, "You don't have to pay me, Mommy!"

Money is a great motivator, especially for young people. Jo and I are convinced that the two most powerful human influences in our lives are the people we meet and the books we read. We can't always control which people we meet, but we can certainly choose the books we read. We wanted to expose our girls to good literature.

During our family nights, as Jo and the girls put together puzzles or coloured Doodle Art pictures, I read many books to them, including C. S. Lewis' *Narnia* series and Tolkien's *The Hobbit* and *The Lord of Rings* trilogy. We wanted our daughters to read other great books for themselves, as well.

When each of our three girls turned 12, we gave them the opportunity to earn some spending money by reading. I posted a list of books, and marked each one with the dollar amount they would earn for reading it. They got part of that money in cash immediately after completing a book, and the other part went into an account for each daughter to spend on whatever she wanted after she had graduated from high school. Whenever they had finished reading a book, I sat down with them to discuss it.

As a result, our teenage girls read scores of excellent motivational and inspirational books, as well as stirring biographies and stimulating true adventures. They already loved books and reading, but still needed that extra motivation—money—to read the books Jo and I wanted them to read.

Money does not just motivate children and teenagers. Several young couples were discussing how they shared the chores around the house. One husband mentioned something that his wife did for him quite regularly. Another husband immediately exclaimed, "You lucky guy! My wife wouldn't do that for love nor money." At that, his wife leaned over to him and said quietly, "You've never tried money."

Many young people already go on short-term mission trips. Some are very successful. For instance, 98 percent of the high school students at our local Christian school were involved in missions one summer, either through their church, with their families or through the school.

Many churches, however, are packed with highly qualified young people who hesitate to leave their comfort zone. Churches, too, could use money to get things started in missions. Perhaps, like little Roger on the waterslide, these young people need some extra motivation—money—to try a cross-cultural foreign missions experience.

What if every church in the country had the following policy? "We will pay for every qualified high school student in our congregation to go abroad one time to do some in-depth, cross-cultural mission work under the auspices of a reputable missions agency."

I suspect many young people currently reluctant to try would accept the offer and return from their first missions experience with beaming faces and with a powerful testimony of how God worked in them and through them.

But they may not be shouting, "You don't have to pay me, church!" since they might want to prepare themselves for a career in missions—a ministry career motivated not by money, but by love for missions and love for the Master of missions. A ministry funded by the Church.

THE ESSENTIAL INGREDIENT FOR SUCCESS

A good business plan, plenty of funding, and well-trained personnel are not enough to accomplish a major task. Success calls for the kind of visionary passion that can overcome mediocre planning, little money and few people.

I know what I am talking about. My wife and I were assigned a huge task. How would we get it done? We had practically no money and no plan to get any. My linguistic studies had produced C grades, although Jo got A's. We had no written work plan beyond going into the Canela village to learn their unwritten language.

In that impoverished state, we arrived at the home of some missionary friends living near a small Brazilian town about 70 kilometres from the Canela village. One evening I was standing in front of their house when my friend joined me. He suddenly grabbed me by the shoulder, pointed down the valley to where a trail came out of the forest, and said, "Look, Jack! Look over there!"

Startled, I turned and saw a dozen men, women and children walking along the valley trail towards town. The men carried muzzle-loading shotguns. Long bush knives dangled from their belts. The women carried baskets on their backs. The men wore shorts, and the women just a piece of cloth wrapped around their hips. The children were naked.

As I stared at this little group, my friend said, "Look, Jack, they are Canelas. They came to trade in town. These are the people you and Jo are going to translate the Bible for!"

"Yes, Lord!" I whispered fervently, as I stretched out my hands toward the Canela going by. "Thank You! Finally we're here. Please help us to reach that village. Help us to make friends with these people. They look rather fierce and unfriendly with their painted bodies and all their weapons.

"Oh God, help us to meet the immediate needs in their village. Help us to learn their language and their culture. Oh God, we need to develop an alphabet and discover the grammar structure of their language. Please help us! How are we going to teach them to read in their own language? And who will help us to translate Your Word? God, please find these helpers, and help us to train them.

"Please God, may those little naked boys and girls someday have Bibles in their homes—ones they can read to their children. Oh God, I don't care what it costs. I don't care what it takes, or how long it takes. Lord, whatever it takes, I'll do it. Please use Jo and me to translate Your Word for these Canela people!"

My face was wet with tears. I surprised myself with the visionary passion I felt.

Twenty-two years later, I stood on the central plaza of that distant Canela village with a newly published partial Bible in my hand, and surrounded by over 1,000 Canelas. Sixty young men and women— graduates of the literacy and Bible memory classes—had earned the right to have a Bible of their own. By the time I had handed out all the Bibles, I was flying high!

Talking with Jo later, I said, "This is one of the greatest days of my life. I am 52 years old, and as far as I am concerned, I could drop dead right now. I don't need to do anything more in this life."

That was nearly 20 years ago, and Jo and I still feel passionate about Bible translation. Some years ago we were on the Singapore-to-London night flight. Wanting to stretch our legs, we walked to the rear exit door and peered out the window as we flew over India.

Ten kilometres below us we could see faint patches of light— villages and small towns—dozens of them. For 25 minutes, as we flew 400 kilometres, we watched that carpet of faint lights flowing endlessly underneath us.

My heart broke as I looked down to villages with hundreds of millions of people desperately needing to know God. I prayed for them, while my eyes stung with tears, blurring the little lights below.

"Lord, there are still thousands of people groups who don't have even one verse of Scripture in the language each knows best—even after all these centuries of Bible translation. Please use Jo and me to do something to bring Your Word to people like these. I don't care what it takes. I don't care what it costs. Lord, whatever it takes, I'll do it. I will speak. I will write. I will travel. I will pray. Just use me, please!"

Jo and I see people with passion all around us. One furlough in Canada, Jo and I visited an elderly friend in her small apartment. The door to her bedroom was partially open, and I happened to notice the bedspread was nearly covered with photographs.

"Are you sorting pictures to put in albums?" I asked.

"No," she said, "Each morning I get up and make my bed. Then I take my box of missionary prayer cards from the dresser and lay all of them out on my bed. I kneel down and pray for some of them and put their cards back in the box. I keep doing that throughout the day and never go to bed until they are all prayed for and back in the box." A passion for prayer.

One of our elderly financial partners lives on one third of his pension income. He gives the other two thirds to missions.

Cardboard boxes are the cabinets to hold his dishes, cutlery and basic food supplies in his little kitchenette. A passion for giving.

A tenured teacher in an African country spoke a tribal language that didn't have any Bible translation. He quit his teaching position, with its guaranteed salary, and joined the Bible translation team to be taught and mentored to translate the Bible for his own people. A passion for service.

The world still needs to be evangelized, the nations to be discipled. What will it take to accomplish this?

A visionary passion in God's people to do whatever it takes.

⁺ COLUMN 41 ⁺
DISCOVERY CHANNEL— CANELA STYLE

Many indigenous societies do not put a high value on privacy. The Canela people, among whom we lived and worked in Brazil for several decades, were one such society.

On Sunday afternoons, Jo and I often hopped on our Honda trail bike and went off to search for personal privacy, blessed silence, restful scenery and a little breeze to keep the biting bugs away.

One day we found these at the top of Rooster Hill, directly east of the village. After an hour, Jo decided to stay to enjoy the scenery some while I went to check out a long line of palm trees in the distance. Palms usually signaled a creek, and there might be a good private swimming hole.

Turned out I would discover something more important than palms and privacy.

I zigged around fallen logs, and zagged around dense clumps of bush, while trying to keep to a general south heading. I also kept alert for possible armadillo burrows and rock-hard termite nests hidden in tall grass. The sky was overcast, but bright, with the sun almost directly overhead. I enjoyed the cooling breeze and the freedom from bugs.

After riding for a while, I began to realize that either those palm trees were a whole lot farther off than I had thought, or I was going in the wrong direction. So as not to worry Jo with my long absence, I turned around and headed back.

I rode north, again zigzagging around obstacles. After a long time, there was Rooster Hill. Or so I thought. When I got a little closer, I saw that it wasn't. "Oh, oh! I'm lost," I thought.

I remembered my survival training, and immediately stopped. My watch reported that it was 12:30 p.m. With the sky brightly overcast and the sun directly overhead, I had no idea which way was north. I would have to wait three hours or more, when the sun would be noticeably in the west and I would be able to get my bearings.

I imagined Jo getting very worried, so I decided to keep riding in the hope of getting somewhere that looked familiar. I rode slowly, constantly scanning for Rooster Hill.

I prayed some, asking God to help me find my way, and to keep Jo from getting worried. I also talked a lot to myself during that time:

"Dummy, why didn't you make sure the compass was in the bike satchel?"

"Any Canela could follow the tire tracks back, even a little kid, why can't you?"

"Why didn't you just sit up there on that hill with Jo and relax, instead of dashing off on this useless trip?"

"Any time now, this bike is going to develop trouble and you'll have to walk out of here."

"Jo is going to be so worried and so angry when you get back… eventually."

I drove about, looking for Rooster Hill for at least an hour—the longest hour of my life.

Suddenly, there it was!

I rejoined Jo at the top of the hill, ready to apologize and explain, but she didn't seem to be upset at my being gone so long.

I looked at my watch. 12:36 p.m. What!

I checked to see if it had stopped, but no, it was still ticking. Only six minutes had gone by since I realized I was lost. It seemed like ten times that long!

That's when I made my discovery. Knowing that you are lost makes the fingers of panic churn your insides. It is hard to stay calm, difficult to think logically, and almost impossible to be objective.

But there is one thing worse than realizing that you are lost. That is to be lost and not know it until it is too late.

Unfortunately, that is exactly the situation for thousands of people groups all over the world. They are stuck in fear-filled cultures and soul-destroying lifestyles, but they know nothing better. They don't know they are lost.

They have no way of learning about God's culture and lifestyle, one that brings peace and gives life in every sense of the word.

These hundreds of millions of people, speaking thousands of different languages, desperately need to have God's Word translated into their languages.

Only then will they have a chance to realize that they are lost and that there is Someone who will point out the way, not just to Rooster Hill, but to a heavenly home.

PEACE IN THE CANDY AISLE

Taking a shortcut from the milk cooler to the cashier, I tried hard to ignore the four-year-old girl who whined and cried her way down the grocery store candy aisle.

Her mother dragged her along by the hand, saying firmly, "No candy right now. We'll be home for dinner soon." The child, an obviously experienced mommy manipulator, suddenly threw herself down on the floor and started screaming. The exasperated mother finally grabbed a candy bar off the store shelf, gave it to her, and peace was restored in the candy aisle.

Peace? Not really. Just until the next time—the next candy aisle, toy store or TV program at bedtime.

The kind of peace that comes from appeasement never lasts. The demands always escalate, whether from a whining four-year-old or a terrorist organization, a recalcitrant union representative or a disgruntled Sunday school teacher.

Societies tend to develop superficial ways of making peace. Take, for instance, the Canela people of Brazil among whom my wife and I lived for many years.

When a conflict breaks out in a Canela village, the way to restore peace is to persuade one of the parties in the conflict to pack up, leave, and let some time go by. Sometimes the person is shamed into going; at other times he or she may leave in a huff. After living in a different village for a few days, a week or even a month or more, the individual or family returns to the home village. No one says anything to anyone about what happened in the past. Time has erased the conflict and restored peace.

Peace? Not really. Just until the next conflict. Instantly all the old enmities spring to life, and the hostility is worse than before. Peace at any price only produces more fuel for the next conflagration. Whining, anger, walking away and passive resistance are destructive ways of dealing with conflict and grudges. They cause time, energy and creativity to be lost in homes, churches, businesses and organizations every day.

Human beings are designed to live, learn and work most productively in peace. And there is a tried and proven way to make peace, true lasting peace.

The ancient prophet Isaiah preached during many years of internal conflict in Jerusalem. He gave the citizens God's recipe for peace: "The work of righteousness shall be peace; and the effect of righteousness quietness and assurance forever" (Isaiah 32:17, KJV).

According to Isaiah, lasting peace does not result from caving in to the person who causes the most trouble, or by walking away in shame or in anger, but by somebody doing the morally and ethically right thing. Peace as a result—a result of morally and ethically right actions—is a repeated biblical theme.

In his famous Sermon on the Mount, Jesus gave clear, easy-to-follow instructions for making peace:

"…If you [recognizing you are not in a right relationship with God] are offering your sacrificial gift at the altar [to show you are sorry and want God to forgive you,] and there remember that your brother [or spouse, fellow worker, etc.] has something against you, leave your gift there in front of the altar. First go and be reconciled to your brother; then come and offer your gift" (Matthew 5:23-24, NIV).

I wonder what would happen in Christian churches around the world this Sunday morning if, during the Prayer of Confession and Pardon, every person who remembered that someone had something against them would get up and walk out to be reconciled? Some pastors might not have many congregants left to hear the sermon. Some congregations might not have a pastor left to preach to them.

What would happen in board meetings, school classrooms and at family dinner tables if no one decided, taught or ate anything until all participants were okay with one another?

Weird? Not at all!

Jesus' recipe for peace tells us to make things right with other people before we make things right with God. That is how this world was designed to operate.

Unless everyone, from leaders to followers, from CEOs to workers, and from parents to children follow the operating instructions in the Manual of Life, no organization, no plant and no home will enjoy true and lasting peace.

Yes, candy aisles and board meetings will quiet down after an appeasement. The fur will stop flying in the factory after one side of a conflict pulls back and keeps a low profile. But unless conflict is taken seriously and dealt with biblically, another ancient prophet's words will be able to describe the situation. He says, "They dress the wound of my people lightly as though it were not serious. 'Peace, peace,' they say, when there is no peace" (Jeremiah 6:14, NIV).

→ COLUMN 43 ←
ME, MYSELF AND I

The cultural anthropologists warned us during our training, "Don't be surprised at how different the Canela will be." But that didn't stop us from being shocked.

We were not surprised by the Canelas' fear of hill demons and ancestral ghosts, or by their wife exchange sex festivals—we expected that sort of thing.

What astonished us was to see the Canela people living together in a more biblically sound way than our friends in the churches back home.

The daily view from our mud-walled house was of Canelas living and working in community. In the morning an extended family of several dozen men, women and children traipses down the trail carrying hoes and bush knives, to work together in their field.

Gangs of young men walk into the bush to chop down trees and dig out the stumps to widen a trail. In the afternoon, groups of girls carry gourds on their shoulders to haul water from the creek. A long line of men and boys drag palm-leaf roofing materials to a house they are building. In the late afternoon the old men sit around their little fire in the central plaza and discuss the day's events, dispense advice and tell stories to the younger men. At sunset a party of hunters returns with armadillos, coatis and a bush deer.

Rarely would we see individuals walk off alone to work. Everything of significance is done in community, in family and in groups.

I have no doubt that God is pleased with this. God created Adam and Eve to be companions for each other. "It is not good for the man to be alone," He said (Genesis 2:18, NIV). He created human beings to work together—to live, communicate, relate and interact in groups.

ME, MYSELF AND I — 161

That is why He is building an international group—His Church—and why He is pleased when His people come together to worship and work together to serve Him.

Unfortunately, during my teen years in the 1950s in western Canada, the churches I attended reflected independence-loving North American culture more than biblical principles. The emphasis was always on the individual acting alone. "Dare to be a Daniel, dare to stand alone," we sang. Sermons and youth pep talks focused on being a lone Christian witness to an antagonistic crowd.

Christians can resist the pressures of our society much more effectively in the company of other believers. God wants us to live, work and witness in community, not in isolation. This biblical focus on community contradicts our own deep-seated, North American concept of rugged individualism and independence.

To ground, nurture and sustain us in today's complicated world, we need to build healthy, interdependent relationships with others. A Zulu proverb says, "A person is not a person without other people."

Jesus defined salvation in terms of restored relationships with God, with ourselves, and with other people. Jesus' high-priestly prayer for the Church was for unity (John 17:21).

Our denominational disunity has for decades damaged our credibility in the eyes of non-Christians. On the other hand, when denominations work together with each other, with missions agencies, and other parachurch organizations—and no one cares who gets the credit—then Christ's prayer is answered and the credibility of the Church is restored.

To fulfill the Great Commission to evangelize the world and disciple the nations, we need to embrace the biblical notion of willing, whole-hearted partnerships with God's people from all over the world. This is happening more than ever on the mission field. For instance, in Wycliffe, the mission agency I know best, 6,000 workers from nearly 50 sending countries work together with another 6,000 people in more than 50 receiving countries. These 12,000 workers represent every kind of national, ethnic, cultural and denominational background, and yet work well together.

In Canada, too, partnerships among churches make possible the operation of major programs such as Alpha that help people learn about the basics of Christianity without a denominational bias.

Summer block parties are often organized and funded by believers in the neighbourhood. Irrespective of what church they attend, they join together with other Christians to make connections with their neighbours, learn each other's names, and start friendships that often lead to sharing their faith.

These efforts help to fight our Western lifestyle and culture, which are so committed to individualism.

The Christian Church in North America needs to learn more about the dynamics of social involvement in the body of Christ. To help us learn we need to ask ourselves questions such as these:

How many good, close friends do I have? The kind that would give me the key to their house or their car if I needed it?

How many people do I have in my life who know everything about me, but accept me anyway?

How many people in my life are willing to confront me about things they feel are wrong with me?

How many non-Christian friends do I have?

How many friends do I have who are not my age, or who are not of my social class?

Is the circle of my close friends growing? Am I flowing into the lives of people?

The Canela people of Brazil do not need to ask themselves these questions. They have always lived life in community. And since receiving God's Word in their own language, many now live life in a community of faith.

And God says, "It is good."

IT NEVER RAINS BUT IT POURS

Life comes at us not in a series of single well-organized events, but in bunches, like flowers in bouquets, or more memorably, like a wheelbarrow load of bricks. It never rains but it pours. Take, for instance, a memorable 24 hours in my life:

A grandchild woke up with an earache, was taken to a clinic, and diagnosed with an ear infection and bronchitis, both conditions needing antibiotics.

The van stalled at the clinic, then was towed back home and parked along the curb to await repairs.

A water leak in the house required two plumbers, who turned off the water for three hours.

The five adults and six children comprising the household were all fully engaged in preparing a birthday party for triplets.

One of the adults was constantly on the phone, trying to organize an unexpected plane flight.

The next morning, well within the 24-hour limit, we discovered that vandals had thrown a fist-sized rock through the van's back window. The van's insurance was at $1,000 deductible.

Those were just the day's highlights (or should I say lowlights?), and this was during our vacation!

It never rains but it pours. It's the experience of people in all cultures and throughout history. No wonder the oldest book of the Bible is the one that tells the story of Job who lost it all in a series of catastrophes—and also tells why.

God designs life to come at us in chunks and bunches.

This flies in the face of current popular psychology that advises us to design a balanced day in order to live a balanced life.* These doctors counsel that each day we need to balance our "shoulds" and our "wants." That is, we need to balance what we should do, usually work-related, with what we want to do, usually hobbies or other recreation.

They caution that doing too much of what you want to do and too little of what you should do might lower your self-esteem, while doing too much of what you should do might make you feel resentful and stress you out. "Balance your day," they say, "and you will balance your life."

Nonsense! The balanced day is a myth. For most active people there is no such thing. Life doesn't happen in nicely balanced daily pieces, nor can it be organized that way. Life is not a balancing act, it is a juggling act. Every good or great thing I have accomplished in my life was done under extremely unbalanced conditions, with intensity, obsession and strong focus—and with joy!

God has something to say about our "shoulds" and our "wants," our self-esteem and the satisfaction we find in work and relationships. For starters, our self-esteem does not depend on doing what we should do, or even on achieving great things. Our self-esteem depends on who we *are*, not on what we *do*. We are children of God. We are loved by the God who is in control of the universe. "Jesus loves me, this I know, for the Bible tells me so." We can do nothing to make Him love us more. A person can be a paraplegic, unable to do anything, and yet have a high self-esteem knowing she is a much-loved child of God.

Secondly, God has given each of His children special talents, unique abilities and spiritual gifts and He calls us to use them in our life and work. We tend to enjoy doing things we do well. God designed us to operate best when our "shoulds" and our "wants" are the same thing. When they are, we do our "shoulds" with deep joy and enormous satisfaction. Obviously the first thing to do is to discover what giftings God has equipped us with, and then design our "shoulds" using those God-given abilities.

My personal "shoulds" call for me to read, observe, think and communicate by writing and speaking. I can do that all day, every day, the more the better. That's why God didn't put me, the Wordman, behind a desk in the finance office! That doesn't mean I neglect financial chores. I struggle, but I do them. We all need to do some things we do not do well and take little joy in, but we must not fill our lives with them.

Our "shoulds" and "wants" cover many areas significant in life: marriage, family, personal development, spiritual growth, physical health, profession, finances and social relationships. No one can keep all these in balance in a day, a week or even a month.

Most realistic is a balanced year! To get something done we need to be ready to live many of our day-to-day lives in unbalanced chunks—obsessively and joyfully going for broke to accomplish something in one area or another.

During our years of work in the Canela village, my wife and I lived an extremely unbalanced life. Our three grade-school daughters boarded in a home with other missionary kids in Belem to study at the Amazon Valley Academy. During those months our family time was zero. Yes, we prayed for them, but that was it. We couldn't even send them a letter.

But did we ever crank out the work! Up at 6 a.m., breakfast, prayers, and at work by 7 a.m. The Canela associates worked with us from 8 a.m. to 5 p.m. with an hour off at noon. A quick bath in the creek on the way back from a jog, a bowl of soup and some crackers for dinner, then back to work again at 7 p.m. teaching a two-hour Bible class, while Jo taught literacy. At 9 p.m., study for an hour or two preparing for the next day's translation work. Routine 80-hour work weeks, month after month. Strong focus on the work? Oh, yes! Joy? You bet! Balance? Forget about it!

On Sundays in the village, we planned family things to do when we got back to our daughters. And when we got back, we did them! Obsessively!

We had nightly family devotions with lots of discussion and stories. Saturday night was family night. No exceptions! Plenty of games and fun. Sunday was family day, with church, exploration drives and picnics, and fun reading in the evening. I read the entire *Hobbit* and *Lord of the Rings* trilogy to the girls while they did crafts. Several weekends at the beach house with fun reading in the evenings.

Saturday morning was family chores. Never mind cutting the grass, chop that bamboo! When the girls turned 12, it was dates with Dad. I set one or two evenings a week aside to take one of my daughters out on a date. When Jo began to feel left out, I added her to the schedule.

Even with the heavy emphasis on family and marriage, our weeks and months during those Belem sessions tended to be more balanced, or, I should say, we juggled more things more successfully.

God loves us, and He is in full control of every day of our lives. That's why we can trust Him to help us deal with the day-to-day stuff in our lives, even when they sometimes land on us like a load of bricks.

*http://www.smartrecovery.org/resources/library/Newsletters/PresidentLetters/jul01.pdf;
    "Booklet 7: Lifestyle balance." http://www.smokefree.gov/pubs/FF7.pdf;
      Marlatt, G. A. "Lifestyle modification." *Relapse Prevention*. Ed. A. Marlatt and J. R. Gordon.
        New York: Guilford, 1985;
      MacPhillamy, D. J., & Lewinsohn, P. M. *Journal of Consulting and Clinical Psychology 50* (1982),
        363–80.

→ COLUMN 45 ←
THE TWO-HANDED GIVER

"Jack," my wife told me one day, "I will let you talk yourself out of a problem you *talked* yourself into, but I won't let you talk your way out of a problem you *behaved* yourself into." It was not the first time she had said this in our 45 years of marriage.

I admit it. When I do something to offend, disappoint or anger someone, my immediate response is to explain and justify myself by using words. The second thing is to apologize, also using words. I have the same instinctive reflex to use words to meet other situations: to comfort people in trouble, to tell funny stories in order to entertain a vanload of bored grandkids, to ask penetrating questions and start an in-depth conversation, or to relate personal anecdotes and encourage a group of teens to get involved in missions.

Using words comes naturally to me. It is a major gift from God.

God creates people with the capacity or talent for developing certain abilities. God's Spirit also gives us one or more strengths in the way we communicate, relate and work. He means for us to develop these natural strengths through training, and then use them to build His kingdom on earth. The Bible mentions at least 18 specific spiritual gifts, of which believers usually have at least one major gift and many other minor ones.

I know some Christians who have a unique combination of spiritual gifts: leadership, administration, wisdom and knowledge. With these abilities they can lead a company to become extremely profitable. Many of these people also have a gift of giving and being sensitive to the needs of others. They are great at funding the kingdom. People with these gifts are able to see business opportunities where anyone else sees only hard work and huge risks.

Some people have the gift of evangelism. They have a highly developed ability to sense when a person not only needs to hear the good news, but is open and ready to listen. Christians who have the gift of evangelism, and are trained in its use, keep meeting people who are ready to listen.

My 94-year-old mother has the gift of helping and serving people. All her life she has wanted to do useful things for others. Nearly 60 years ago, amid the crowds of immigrants on a dock in Halifax, she sat on a suitcase and breastfed a baby whose distraught mother had lost her milk. Even now, her numerous great-grandsons wear pants with knees that she keeps patched. Daily she visits and reads to bedridden friends in her retirement lodge. Christians with the gift of service keep seeing things they can do for people.

It seems God gives talents, abilities and spiritual gifts to His people with one hand, and with the other hand He gives opportunities to use them. And He expects us to take the opportunities and use the gifts He gives us.

On Popjes family workdays, one grandchild gets a shovel, another a rake, and another an axe. I then assign one to dig a flowerbed, another to rake leaves, and another to split kindling. With one hand I give the tools, with the other I indicate the opportunity to use them. How ridiculous would it be if I expected all three to use their specific tools to do all three jobs? How could they split wood with the shovel or rake with the axe? In the same way, God gives us the tools with one hand and points out the work with the other.

You would think, therefore, that everyone would find out what their talents, gifts and abilities are as soon as possible, and then develop them through training and use. Unfortunately that is not always what happens.

I have heard preachers, read authors, and sat under teachers who pushed the idea that every Christian should share the good news with every person he or she meets, and be a prayer warrior, and be a sympathetic counsellor, and help others, and be an encourager, and start new ministries, and lead, and be this, and do that, and, and, and.

I have seen Christians struggling to do jobs they were "guilted" into doing, but for which they had no strengths and no spiritual gifts. Naturally, they felt like losers, like the proverbial square pegs in round holes.

We all know that every job will have some components that don't fit the strengths of the worker, but we should not spend our whole workday operating in our area of weakness.

Gifted people, working in their areas of strength, are the best builders of God's worldwide kingdom. Churches under good leadership and reputable missions agencies such as Wycliffe know this to be true. That is why they insist that the people who serve in their organizations know what their strengths and abilities are, and then help them to choose an area of ministry where they can shine.

God designed people to work at positive, up-building activities. He intends us to work hard, so that we are physically tired at the end of a workday. But He does not want us to be emotionally exhausted. Yet that will be the result if we insist on working consistently outside our areas of strength.

When I do "word work," I can go day and night and not be exhausted emotionally. When I attempt to do "number work," I am emotionally spent before I even find my calculator.

We need to encourage each other to discover how God has gifted us and work as much as possible in those areas of strength. We will work hard and feel physically tired, but we will also be emotionally energized by the sense of accomplishment at the end of the day.

→ COLUMN 46 ←
AXE HEAD AND HANDLE:
A VITAL PARTNERSHIP

Few missionaries are linguistic geniuses. Jo and I certainly are not. For us, translating the Bible without a fluent speaker of the target language as a constant partner would be like chopping wood with only an axe handle.

That is why, as soon as we arrived in the Canela village in Brazil, we looked for Canela people who would help us learn the language so we could analyze it and develop a writing system. After that, we looked for Canela people who were great storytellers and communicators, so we could train them and work with them as partners to translate God's Word into Canela. Bible translation was our main task since it is closest to God's own heart. At least that is what I understand David to say in Psalm 138:2, when he writes, "You have magnified Your word above all Your name" (NKJV).

After our first year of living in the Canela village, we noticed a new face on the block. Jaco, a teenager, had just returned from spending years in the big city. He was one of a group of Canelas who fled the village during an attempted massacre some years before we arrived. He had attended school in the city and learned to read and write in Portuguese.

Jaco was bright and highly motivated to learn, so we invited him to work with us. Soon he learned to touch-type on our old Underwood and transcribed Canela stories and linguistic material faster and more accurately than I could. Unfortunately, having been away from the village for years, he was not as fluent in Canela, nor did he have as large a vocabulary as other young people his age. He was, therefore, unsuitable to partner with us in translation, and we kept praying and looking for someone. God, however, had plans for Jaco.

After a few months' break in the city, Jo and I returned to the village to discover that Jaco was "in seclusion." The village elders had decided that since he had not gone through the puberty rites as a child, he needed to go through them now, along with all the much younger boys.

I went to talk with him that same evening. I found him shut up alone in a small seclusion hut behind his relatives' house. Just like all the other initiates, he was not allowed to talk, work or sing—just silence, solitude and no physical labour.

We whispered to each other through the thatch. "I am so bored," he complained. "I wish I was back with you working on making reading books. But the elders won't let me go out or do any work."

He would be there for at least three months, receiving his food through a little slot in the palm-thatch wall. This is meant to teach young Canelas to get along without fire, clothing, covering or human companionship, and with only a small amount of water and food. The hardships they endure during this time make them into true Canelas, able to sleep under any conditions and get along with only the very basic necessities of life.

The next day I asked permission to speak to the elders at their early morning council session. "Every evening, when you tell stories of the old days, I have heard you complain that the young people are not coming to listen. You worry that after you are dead, no one will remember the stories. I have been making books of a few of your stories. Would you like all your stories to be in books? If they were, your descendants could read them forever."

"Yes, that's true," the elders replied, "but we are too old to learn to write down our stories."

"But you could tell more stories to my tape recorder, and then someone else, like Jaco, could quietly listen to them with headphones and copy them on the typewriter. That way we could make books from them for your grandchildren to read."

They discussed it for a while and gave their verdict: "Listening to stories on the headphones doesn't make noise, and tap-tapping them on the typewriter isn't work, so go ahead and ask Jaco to do this."

A few nights later, Jaco began what turned out to be his formal education as a Bible translation partner. For three full months, he did nothing but listen to stories told by the best storytellers in the village. In listening and typing the hundreds of pages of text, he developed a powerful vocabulary, an excellent sense of language style, and a deep appreciation for the subtleties of his own language. When he finally came out of seclusion, God had shaped him into an excellent partner for us as translators of God's Word into Canela.

With his fluency in Canela fitted to our knowledge of the Bible and our access to translation consultants, we became a perfect team—a sharp axe head fitted tightly to a strong handle. Twenty years later we completed the partial Bible translation project.

God continues to choose and prepare thousands of men and women all over the world. They are joining Bible translation teams in over 1,000 different cultures.

Some indigenous translation partners, like our friend and co-worker Jaco, are fluent in their own language but have only a basic general education. Increasingly, however, in more developed countries, nationals on translation teams are better educated. Some are even linguistic geniuses, fluent in many languages, with Ph.D.s from prestigious universities.

No matter what their background, they have one thing in common: God Himself chose and prepared them to help accomplish His world goal—speakers of every language in the world hearing His good news in the languages each of them knows best.

Just as He prepares these axe heads, so He prepares the axe handles—the translation consultants, the specialists in computers, in literacy, in anthropology, in funding and in management.

God's Spirit inspired people to write His Word, and now He is preparing people and helping them to translate His Word into every human language. God is the Main Partner.

Two thousand Bible translation projects to go.

→ COLUMN 47 ←
THE ORIGINAL CODE—REBOOT

It happened to me again just now—not the first time this week either. I use my computer many hours a day, flipping from one to another of five or six programs all running at once. Then, suddenly, the keyboard goes dead. I click on a file but it just won't open. My computer does that a couple of times a week.

I used to fuss and mess around, try this and that and, in general, lather myself into a state of frustration. Not anymore. I just close as many programs as I can and shut down the computer. Sometimes I have to do drastic things, like unplug my laptop and take out the battery. Then I start it up again and…ta-da! Everything works as it should…until the next time.

Bill, my Wycliffe colleague, mentor and rescuer of all things computerish, once explained to me what happens, using biblical terminology usually reserved to describe extremely bad people. No, not the theological expressions one hears from the unregenerate under these frustrating conditions, but biblical nonetheless.

"Sometimes lines of code in a program become corrupt and no longer function as they should," he said. He went on to explain that these corrupt files are unfixable, and the only thing a person could do is replace them with clean, uncorrupted originals. The way to do that is to reboot—shut down the computer and then start it up again.

God faced this situation and took a similar action several times. Genesis 6:11–12 says, "The earth also was corrupt before God, and the earth was filled with violence. And God looked upon the earth, and, behold, it was corrupt; for all flesh had corrupted his way upon the earth" (KJV). He sent the flood, shutting down life on earth, and rebooted.

The nation of Israel throughout their long history corrupted themselves repeatedly by abandoning the original code and worshipping idols instead of God. God looked at Israel and saw that they were corrupt and unfixable. So God shut down the nation in Palestine. He sent Israel into exile and rebooted 70 years later.

Even today, we humans continue to corrupt our lines of code—no amount of tweaking can fix us. We need rebooting.

That is why God sent Jesus, the uncorrupted Original, to take our place, and to replace our corrupt programming through His Holy Spirit. This alone is a great devotional thought, but there is more.

From time to time, you and I act like computers. We think all the time, we talk constantly, and we work long hours every day. And then, suddenly—speaking for myself—I lose it. I say something I should not have said. My hearers are offended. My wife is hurt, disgusted, upset. You name it. I messed up.

When that happens, I need to realize some coding inside my inner computer has become corrupt—has changed from the original. It is not fixable. It needs to be replaced. How do I reboot? I stop what I am doing and go for a walk or take a break. I take myself off-line and take time to shut down my inner computer. I take time to repent, confess and make things right. In other words, I ask Jesus to reprogram me with His original coding.

Sometimes my loving, perceptive wife can sense the initial corruption of a malfunctioning line of code in my inner computer. "Go for a walk by yourself," she'll say, and then she will softly mutter, "You need it." She is right. I need periodic time off-line. Maybe you do too.

If I were running the world, I would mandate a whole day off-line for everyone on a regular basis—time off to reboot our inner computers.

Like once a week.

It would be time to just stop, unplug ourselves from all but our essential duties, and get reprogrammed.

That would be so good for humanity.

Hmm, didn't Someone recommend that already in His "ten commandments"?

LONGINGS INDESCRIBABLE

A Canela friend visited our home at the mission centre, sat down on a rocking chair, and startled himself when he leaned back. From then on a rocking chair was known as the "eye-widener." The word for *jeep* or *truck* in Canela is "big-rubber-travel-thing." When Canelas return to their jungle village from visiting the city, they struggle to describe what their hearers have never seen or experienced.

So it was when the old apostle John tried to describe what he saw in his visions of heaven and the earth's future. Nearly 100 times he uses the words *like* and *as* to describe his experience. For example, he uses phrases such as "eyes like a flame of fire," "a voice as of a trumpet," "feet like molten brass," "as it were the noise of thunder," and "tails like serpents."

We, just like Canela villagers, have a hard time picturing the reality of what is being described.

I suspect that when it comes to heaven, our North American culture consistently guesses wrong. The cartoonist drawing a white-robed saint looking bored as he sits on a cloud, strumming a little harp, does not match what the Bible teaches about the afterlife. Neither do the jokes about Saint Peter at the Pearly Gates or the stories about pleasures such as unlimited golf on the perfect course.

The apostle John did his best to sketch the picture, yet I am inclined to think that our imaginings fall far short of the reality. I have read a lot of science fiction, so I know how to use my imagination. Even so, my ideas about heaven are probably pale, watery imitations of what eternity is really like. Certainly we will worship in heaven. But how? By singing all the time? I doubt it. Even here on earth we worship God in multiple ways: by serving Him with the best work of which we are capable, by meeting the needs of other people as

God leads and equips us, by joining together with other believers, and by helping each other to live out our faith in our own individual ways.

No human being has ever seen, heard or even imagined what God has prepared for those who love Him. So Saint Paul tells the church in Corinth (1 Corinthians 2:9). On that basis we can let our imaginations loose on what eternity with God will be like.

My imagination is often driven by an indescribably strong longing, a craving to experience something that would be totally impossible for me on earth. As I take in the vista of a vast mountain, I hunger to be an eagle swooping along the glistening snow cap and down the rocky side into the warm, green valley. I watch a thunderstorm approach and crave to be part of that cloud, part of the flashing lightning bolt.

The lifelong friendship of the Billy Graham core team and their incredible close working relationship makes my heart ache with unfulfilled yearning.

When I read master authors, watch Olympic athletes, and listen to professional orchestras, not only do I enjoy the experience, but I want to be the writer, be the athlete, and be the musician.

Sometimes my mind goes into hyperdrive and does a faster-than-the-speed-of-light jump into outer space. "Zillions of stars" is how one NASA website cites the number of stars in the universe. So enormous, so ancient, so immense, and all created by our God who is immeasurably greater than His creation. How I would love to travel among all those galaxies!

C. S. Lewis once wrote that "if I find in myself a desire which no experience in this world can satisfy, the most probable explanation is that I was made for another world."* C. S. Lewis has it right.

Someday, God will complete his plan for the planet Earth and all the people on it. He will make it all new, and we too will be made anew. We will have utterly new bodies. We will live as individuals who can be part of the beauty we now just admire. We will be able to truly know and love, not just a few close friends, but everyone. And they will know us and love us.

What a staggering difference between the future of the Christian believer and that of those who believe that death ends it all. Or those who can only hope to be absorbed into the All, losing their individuality in the process. Or those who see human life as an endless cycle of deaths and births. Or those whose heaven is a place filled with male-oriented earthly pleasures.

Just think: All 6,501,687,745 people living on earth today were made for another world. Each man and woman of these billions has desires that can only be satisfied there, but only one out of five has read Saint John's description of that future world. Relatively few know how to fully share in it through faith in Jesus and in what He has done for them.

That is what keeps driving us on to evangelize the world and disciple the nations through the Word of God, translated into every language on earth.

*Lewis, C. S. *Mere Christianity*. New York: Macmillan, 1952, 120.

I SPY WITH MY LITTLE EYE

My wife and I often play a game with our grandkids when driving about the city. We've all played it as kids ourselves, or with our children or grandchildren. Someone says, "I spy with my little eye, I see something...*red*!" Then we all look around and suddenly red objects pop out everywhere and the guessing begins.

While traveling in a van for six weeks with some young actors, I played the grown-up version of this game: "I spy with my little eye, I see something...*God*." I put it in a slightly different form, asking each one, "Where did you see God in the last 24 hours?"

Suddenly God things were popping out everywhere. The answers were as varied as the personalities and backgrounds of each of the young people.

"The beauty, majesty and silence of last night's sunset reflected the peace of God in my heart."

"The smile of a baby I saw at lunch yesterday, a baby made in the image of God."

"The power of the waves on Lake Superior, created by my God."

"I sat beside a pond in the moonlight enjoying the stillness and solitude, and I sensed God's still, small voice in my mind."

We tend to see what we are looking for; we tend to be blind to everything else. A big-game photographer visited northeast India where he photographed dozens of tigers. On the flight home, he sat next to a Christian missionary from the same part of India. The photographer scornfully remarked that he had been in India for four months and had never seen a Christian church, implying that the missionary's work had had little effect. The missionary replied, "I have lived in villages in northeast India for 40 years and have never seen a tiger."

If you are "spying with your little eye" for evidence of sin among Christians, you will find tons of it. There are no flawless people, no, not even among Christians. Some of us sin secretly in our minds and imaginations. Others carry the evidence out in front of themselves where everyone can see it. Like me with my "eat too much and exercise too little" belly.

On the other hand, if we look for evidence of holy living among Christians, we will also find plenty. I recently preached at a new church plant in San Jose, California. Wanting to help the homeless in the area, the congregation collected hundreds of small items useful for homeless people, such as food, a pocket Bible, hygiene products, etc. The children decorated white paper bags with crayon art and packed them. Now every vehicle in the congregation has a little stack of bags to hand out when they "spy" a homeless person holding up his sign at an intersection. Practical holiness.

This same church is organizing their volunteers on a skills database. When needy people come to church and ask for help, a volunteer with the right skill set is assigned to help them. Christ followers.

Back in Canada one of our daughters told us about a neighbouring family that took a six-week-long break from work and school over the Christmas holidays. At their own expense, they traveled to a developing country and worked in an orphanage. A Christmas present to Jesus.

Our little grandson, Aidan, was invited to a friend's birthday party with instructions not to bring a present but to bring money to help poor people. The birthday gift money was collected and sent to a relief and development agency to help a destitute family in Africa.

A gift catalogue circulated around the Christian school our grandkids attend, and the idea made an impact. A few months later, it was our grandson's seventh birthday. "I already have lots of toys," he said. "I want to buy a goat for some boy in Africa." Little Saint Aidan.

If you "spy with your little eye" for evidence of government mismanagement, or unfair wages in business, or greed in industry, you will see it everywhere.

On the other hand, if the object of the game is to look for new legislation to protect children from exploitation, or for businesses that provide free care for employees' elderly parents, and for pharmaceutical companies whose products save or improve multi-millions of lives around the globe, you will be overwhelmed with evidence.

Saint Paul didn't use the "I spy with my little eye" metaphor, but he could have when he advised the church in the city of Philippi to fill their minds with "…things true, noble, reputable, authentic, compelling, gracious—the best, not the worst; the beautiful, not the ugly; things to praise, not things to curse" (Philippians 4:8, *The Message*).

A good place to start meditating is on Paul's piece of advice. Let's face it, from time to time we all need an attitude tune-up.

We need to recalibrate our mind and refocus "our little eye."

JESUS' BIRTHDAY PRESENT

I was a deprived child. Yes, believe it or not, I was 12 years old before I received my first Christmas present.

It's true. I am not making this up.

I can already hear many of you exclaim as you grope for your chequebook, "Oh that poor boy! Let's send him some money to make up for all those years of not getting any Christmas presents!"

Great idea! But before you do, I should give you this little explanation.

I grew up in the Netherlands where mid winter gift giving is not done at Christmas, but three weeks earlier on the birthday of Saint Nicholas. I learned to love this bishop as *Sinterklaas*, about whom I sang songs with my friends and family, and who left us gifts in the wooden shoes I had carefully placed by the fireplace on the night of December 5.

Christmas, therefore, was totally given over to remembering the birth of Jesus with no gift giving involved at all. It seems that the Dutch and the Flemish are unique in this practice. (They are unique in many other ways too, highly intelligent, incredibly handsome, hardworking and, of course, extremely humble. But we won't go into that just now.)

When we emigrated to Canada, our parents took a dim view of mixing Christmas and presents. They felt it was somewhat sacrilegious and detracted from the meaning of Christmas. And that was half a century before the modern, commercialized shopping frenzy that threatens to eclipse the celebration of our Saviour's birth today.

On the other hand, there is something very appropriate about celebrating the birth of Christ by giving gifts. Jesus Himself was God's gift to mankind—the greatest gift of all. The wise men brought

Him three gifts. In many cultures of the world, people celebrate the birthdays of friends and relatives by giving them presents.

But don't you find it a little odd to celebrate someone's birthday by giving presents to each other, and not to the person whose birthday it is? I doubt Jesus is positively impressed with the 35 billion dollars' worth of presents that are exchanged in His name on His birthday.* What does impress Him, however, is what many Christians are doing.

Remember the "grope for your chequebook" attempt at humour a few paragraphs ago? Here is the serious side.

Groping for our chequebook is exactly what Jo and I, and a growing number of Christians, do at this time of year. They count up how much money they spend on presents to each other, and then give a similar amount to benefit the desperately poor around the world.

Conservatively estimating one out of ten North Americans to be Christians, if we Christians did this, over three billion dollars would be sent to make a noticeable impact in meeting extreme world needs.

It's a biblically sound policy too. One day, Jesus told an end-of-the-world story about people who in their life on earth had helped the poor, fed the hungry and cared for the sick and the homeless. At the end He concluded, "…Whatever you did for one of the least of these brothers of mine, you did for me" (Matthew 25:40, NIV).

Use your money this Christmas to help someone who is in financial need and is therefore physically, emotionally or spiritually deprived.

It will be your birthday present to Jesus. He'll be pleased!

---

*Antrim, Kathleen. "Everyone benefits from 'Christmas.'" *The Examiner*. 7 December, 2006. http://www.kathleenantrim.com/54.html.

MARY'S BOY CHILD

Music speaks directly to the emotions, bypassing the brain. That is its power. But some lyrics speak clearly to our minds even as the music strongly affects our emotions. Two songs are guaranteed to do that for me, especially at the Christmas season. The lyrics confirm my faith. The music rouses my emotions, lifting my heart to worship in spirit and in truth—even as tears slide down my face.

I sang bass in a Bible college choir that performed some of Handel's *Messiah* every year. Even though I have heard or sung it hundreds of times, I still tend to cry my way through the "Hallelujah Chorus" whenever I hear it sung or played. One year, Jo and I experienced those emotions from our fifth-level gallery as we listened to a master performance of *Messiah* by the Edmonton Symphony Orchestra and Choir. But I can be stirred by the music even without formal, beautiful surroundings.

I remember the last few hours of a muddy, four-day motorcycle trip to Belem, Brazil, from Brasilia where I had left the final manuscript of the partial Bible translated into Canela with the printer. Through earphones I listened to music on my Walkman cassette player tucked into an inside pocket. When the "Hallelujah Chorus" started, I, with voice breaking from emotion, bellowed along with the choir:

King of kings, and Lord of lords!
And He shall reign forever and ever!
Hallelujah! Hallelujah!

There is nothing quite like Handel to bring tears to my eyes and a catch to my voice—unless it is Boney M*, a 1980's Caribbean vocal group accompanied by steelpan and other percussion instruments.

The lyrics of one of their Christmas songs start off rather innocuously:

Sometime ago in Bethlehem, so the Holy Bible say,
Mary's boy child, Jesus Christ, was born on Christmas day.
Hark now hear the angels sing, a King was born today,
And man will live forevermore because of Christmas day.

A few lines follow about the shepherds and angel choirs, and their search for the Baby; then:

And then they found in a little nook, in a stable all forlorn,
In a manger cold and dark, Mary's little boy was born.

Steelpan music and kettledrums join voices humming in close harmony. Then the ending: just the thump, thump of the drum, with all four voices in harmony singing a great prayer of praise:

Oh my Lord, You sent Your Son to save us.
Oh my Lord, Your very self You gave us.
Oh my Lord, that sin may not enslave us,
and love may reign once more.

This day will live forever, Oh praise the Lord.
He is the Truth forever, Oh praise the Lord.
His light is shining on us, Oh praise the Lord.
He is the jubilation, Oh praise the Lord.
Until the sun falls from the sky, this day will live forever.

What makes me blubber all the way through those lines? The sure and certain knowledge that someday, when all the earthly practicing is done, we will sing truths like these in the great heavenly choir.

It won't be a choir of white Anglo-Saxon Protestants in formal suits and black dresses. We will join a vast multitude from every language, every race and every people group. We will sing together with them the greatest lyrics in the universe.

With bursting hearts, we will praise God for sending His only Son to be born as a human baby, to live a holy life on earth, to die in our place, and then to come alive again to bring us everlasting life.

We will sing lyrics not to build our faith, but to celebrate its fulfillment.

*Boney M. *Christmas Album*, 1981.

Michael, the Real Christmas Angel

That first Christmas was so ordinary. Yes, even a bit "ho-hum." We have heard the familiar story over and over again. We have sung about it repeatedly and watched numberless Christmas plays—almost to the point of boredom.

It was all so very human, so very common. Look at these everyday, commonplace elements: a busy innkeeper bustling about; a worried husband doing his best to prepare a bed, making do with the best of what is left; a young pregnant woman starting labour; tired donkeys resting while their owners sleep; some simple shepherds watching for ewes about to give birth.

It was all so human, so earthy, so predictable and so utterly normal. All is calm; peace on earth.

Oh yeah?

What do you think this looked like from a cosmic, God-oriented view? The birth of Jesus was an invasion—a one-man invasion, or rather a one-God invasion, with nothing like peace and calm about it!

Check out the elements listed symbolically in Revelation 12. There's nothing simple and human about these! Instead of a humble, pregnant peasant girl, here is a woman—symbolizing the nation of Israel—about to give birth to a King who would rule the nations with immense power, symbolized by an iron scepter.

Instead of tired donkeys, here is a ferocious dragon, symbolizing Satan, ready to devour the Child as soon as He is born! Instead of wondering shepherds silently kneeling around a manger, here are armies of angels and demons at war. Instead of Gabriel leading an angel chorus singing praises, here is Michael leading his angel armies to victory in Heaven, and violently evicting Satan and his armies.

This war continues on earth. We, God's people, are His armies, battling in prayer against enemies in the spiritual realm. We struggle against every kind of opposition to spread the good news of God's love and the gift of His Son. We work hard to evangelize the world and disciple the nations.

We all know churches that reach out into the community to bring people the good news. We have heard of Bible translators and other missionaries who reveal God to people by giving them His Word in a familiar language. We read dozens of stories of the newly translated Word coming to people groups for the first time.

It is all so very human, so very common. Look at these everyday, commonplace elements: Young men and women train to be translators, leave home, spend years learning the language and the culture, write letters home, receive cheques from supporters, figure out an alphabet, suffer loneliness, train others, deal with sickness, check manuscripts, teach, translate, age, and on and on. Finally the Word is published, joyous celebrations are held, and new churches are grown. During the past 70 years it has been done over 1,000 times. It is all so human, so earthy, so predictable and so utterly normal.

Oh yeah?

What do you think this looks like from a cosmic, God-oriented view? No, it doesn't look like just one more translation program, but like an invasion into Satan's territory. An angelic army backs up the small team of human liberators fighting their way through the defenses of the occupying forces.

Fierce battles break out and Satan counterattacks as he sees his traditional hold on hidden peoples and cultures begin to loosen. Violent conflicts erupt in unearthly places for the souls of men and women, who, for the first time, are beginning to catch a glimpse of a spiritual world they never knew existed. Then, as their ferocious age-old Enemy is beaten back, the liberated people groups move from fearing demons and evil spirits to trusting a loving heavenly Father.

Gabriel is a mere messenger. The great archangel Michael is the real Christmas angel. He is the commanding general of God's invading armies in the continuing cosmic battle that started at the first Christmas. And all humans have a part in this battle.

Now that is exciting! Just as God chose Mary to give birth to the Living Word of God so that He would be revealed to all mankind, so He chooses us to bring the written Word to all the people groups of the world.

Most of what we see around us with our physical eyes is transitory. The only things permanent and eternal are the Word of God and the souls of people.

That is why we look around with the eyes of faith. We continue to work and to struggle, knowing that what we do in God's power here on earth has significant, eternal consequences in the permanent world inhabited by God and His angelic armies.

Celebrate the great invasion this Christmas.

→ COLUMN 53 ←
THE MAIN CHARACTER
IN THE STORY OF MY LIFE

The main character in the story of "The Life of Jack Popjes" is not a person named Jack. The longer I live, the clearer this becomes.

For the past few years, I have been studying the art of writing stories for children (which is harder than writing for adults, by the way). As I studied, I began to see my own life's story in terms of such narrative basics as character growth, structure outline and plot development.

That's when it hit me in a new way—I am not the main character in my life's story. Not only am I not the main character, but my life story is not the main story!

The Main Character (and it's about time I started to use capitals) invited me to play a part in His Story—a small part—a minor character in the Great Story of which He is both the Author and the Main Character.

At 70 years old, I regret that I didn't fully realize all this right from the start of my Christian life. I can't count the number of times I lived as though I was the main character in my life, an attitude that really screwed things up.

Since Jo and I were the only people fluent in the Canela language who also had a thorough understanding of the Bible, I used to think that we were, therefore, the key persons in the Canela Bible translation program. It took 12 years, some messed-up relationships, and months of depression before I posted a small sign on my translation desk which read, "The only Person indispensable to the Canela Bible translation program is Jesus Christ."

Since God had called Jo and me to the task of translating the Bible for the Canela, I used to think that, therefore, the Wycliffe organization in Canada and its sister organization in Brazil existed to help us to do our task. My view was that if these organizations failed to help us, they failed God.

You can imagine how unimpressed the leadership of the Brazil organization was with me. It took a decade of hard times before I realized I was part of a large team of workers in which each was expected to help the other person, even if it meant progress on his own work had to stop for a while. Many years later I played a leadership role in Brazil, and later in Wycliffe Canada—experiences that helped me see how small my role was then, and continues to be now.

Until our first furlough, I used to think that churches back in North America were "geese to be plucked" and that we missionaries should not shirk our responsibility to shake people and money out of the church in order to mobilize them to evangelize the world. We felt the burden of world evangelization was on our shoulders and the churches should be helping us.

But eventually, to my great relief, I began to realize that neither I nor my fellow missionaries were responsible to evangelize the world and disciple the nations. God had given that responsibility to the worldwide Church. The churches were not there to help the missionaries; we missionaries were there to help the churches. God Himself would hold church leaders accountable for any delay in carrying out the cross-cultural, foreign missions task.

Even today, I frequently think that besides my ministry work, words and worries, I am the one solely responsible for the success of my marriage, family and relationships. I see myself as the main character of the story, totally responsible to solve problems, satisfy everyone, set the goals and attain them.

All hogwash, of course!

I am part of a Great Story that started long ago, before the creation of the world—a Story that will go on into eternity. In comparison to the overall plot, my life is, as the biblical poet said, merely a momentary vapour.

It is short, but not without significance.

The Author and Main Character invited me to play a small but important part in His Great Story. He designed me before I was born, imprinted my DNA and my personality with all its strengths and weaknesses. He planted the seed of Himself within me and is growing me into the likeness of His Son, Jesus. Someday, the sooner the better, I will be fully like Him!

What's true for me is, of course, true for my wife, Jo, and for every God worshipper. The Great Story is about Him. As we pay attention to the Author of the Story—the Director of the play—our small but important part in the Great Story will develop in the direction He wants it to go.

He puts us into situations that develop our characters. He surrounds us with other characters, who are all equally invited to play a part in His Story. He lays out the overall plans and prepares us so we can play our parts well. His written Word sets the standards for our lives. He gives us His Spirit to guide and empower us to live our part in the Great Story.

It's not all about me. What a relief!

ABOUT JACK POPJES

Born in Holland, Jack immigrated with his family to Canada in 1950. He attended Berean Bible College in Calgary. Jack and Jo were married in 1962 and pastored a Baptist church in Innisfail, Alberta, for three years before joining Wycliffe in 1965. They left for Brazil in 1966 with three preschool daughters and began work with the Canela people in 1968.

When the Popjeses began their work, the Canela people were illiterate and there were no Christian believers. By the time the Scriptures in the Canela language were dedicated in 1990, there were many Canela believers, all able to read the Bible and teach others to read and obey the Word.

After the Popjeses left Brazil in 1990, they served with Wycliffe Canada and spoke at many conferences and banquets.

Jack served as CEO for Wycliffe Canada for six years, beginning in 1994. He led the organization through many changes in preparation for service in the new millennium. Jack was then appointed CEO of Wycliffe Caribbean with a mandate to restructure the organization, and find and train a successor. He completed this task in May 2004.

Currently Jack is the Wycliffe Canada national representative, serving as a speaker and writer.

CONTACT

You may contact the author utilizing the following methods:

#402, 1 Spruce Ridge Drive
Spruce Grove, AB, T7X 4N4   ive   Canada
Email: jack_popjes@wycliffe.ca   N4
http://popjesthemandate.blogspot.com   ail, send a blank email
http://insightsandoutbursts.blogspot.com

Check the author's website (www.thewordman.ca) for archived articles, speaking calendar and more information about the author and his family.

To order additional copies of this book contact the Wycliffe Media Resource Center by calling 1-800-WYCLIFFE or email mrco@wycliffe.org to place your order.

To order an autographed copy of this book, contact the author directly.